Passionate and Compassionate Love

Passionate and Compassionate Love

A Vision for Christian Marriage

JACK DOMINIAN

Darton, Longman and Todd
London

First published in 1991 by
Darton, Longman and Todd Ltd
89 Lillie Road, London SW6 1UD

ISBN 0-232-51934-X

A catalogue record of this book is available from the British Library

Phototypeset by
Intype, London
Printed and bound in Great Britain by
Courier International Ltd, East Kilbride

Contents

Part III *Issues for the Christian Community*

Preface

In 1981 my book *Marriage, Faith and Love* was published. It presented an up-to-date view of contemporary marriage and its links to faith through love. The book was kindly received and gained wide publicity. Ten years later it was out of print. I was faced with a dilemma. I had the choice of writing a second, enlarged edition, or retaining its central findings and rewriting it. I decided in favour of the latter.

In the course of the last ten years I have lectured widely in the British Isles and abroad, and have developed a new approach to the subject which is more comprehensive, coupled with a clearer presentation of the topic.

At the heart of the book remain three themes. The first one is that we are in the midst of a social revolution in which marriage is shifting from a traditional form which has prevailed for the last hundred years to a relationship of love. This secular shift, which is hard to detect because we are in the middle of it, is coinciding with a religious view which also treats marriage and the family as a community of love. There is thus a challenge of how to reconcile the two approaches so that society and the Christian community engage in a common venture. Secondly, it is important for the churches to recognise that marriage is the principal way through which the majority of human beings experience God, in so far as God is love. There is a deep sense of urgency for Christianity to put marriage on the map and to show that in this community of love God is to be found.

Coupled with a reinforcement of the significance of marriage, we need to restore the unique importance of sexuality. Sexuality has had poor treatment at the hands of Christianity for the whole of its duration. Sex was made respectable by linking it to procreation. Today the overwhelming majority of sexual activity is non-procreative, and a new meaning has to be found for this precious gift from God.

Thus the three themes are: the understanding of marriage as a community of love; that it is through this love that the overwhelming majority of human beings find God; and that sexuality and love are linked in a vital way.

Those who possess copies of *Marriage, Faith and Love* will find the new version a highly developed enterprise; and those unacquainted with it will discover my thoughts, developed over thirty years, contained in this book. Essentially marriage will be described as a secular reality taken up in the Lord and made into a divine mystery.

No references are given in this book, but anyone interested can write to me and I will provide the details. The reason for not giving references is that, while the book is based extensively on research findings and my own clinical observations, it was not written as a scientific documentation: this will be the subject of a separate publication. I want as many people as possible to read this book unburdened by the cluttering of scientific references.

JACK DOMINIAN

Part I

Focus on Love

1

The Centrality of Love

For most of us one of the central experiences of our life is our childhood, during which we received the essentials of love. These essentials depend on the fact that we spent nearly two decades dependent for our survival and development on our parents. Modern psychology is in the process of analysing this period and discovering that the secret of life is to be found in a combination of the genes with which we were endowed and the experiences we received from our father and mother. It is no exaggeration to state that these two decades unfold for us the mystery of life, and this mystery is to be found in one word, which is love. This love is experienced in the first relationship of intimacy in our childhood, and courtship and marriage brings us into the second, exclusive, attachment of intimacy. Thus love experienced in and through intimacy links our childhood with our adult life.

At the heart of the Christian faith is also to be found the centrality of love, and one of the purposes of this book is to show that marital love constitutes for most human beings their central experience of God, and their most precious neighbour is first their spouse, then their children, and finally the neighbour who is near or far away. There is a great danger in contemporary society to miss this point. It is missed by the secular world which sees marriage as a mere contract with social implications, and by Christianity which recognises marriage as a sacrament, but does very little to help Christians see its vital importance in their life. The secular world can be forgiven for mistaking marriage for a mere contract, but even here we shall see that it is moving in the direction of appreciating the importance of love in it. But Christianity

3

has no excuse, for love has featured centrally in its revelation throughout the Judaeo-Christian tradition. It will be argued by critics of this view that the love of the Scriptures, particularly of the New Testament, is that of agape, not eros. But this is a false distinction because, as we shall see, marital love encompasses both falling in love and loving. Marital love is love of neighbour, and scriptural love is love of neighbour.

Love of neighbour is to be found in the law of Moses, the essentials of which are written in the Book of Leviticus:

When you reap the harvest of your land, you will not reap to the very edges of the field, nor will you gather the gleanings of the harvest; nor will you strip your vineyard bare, nor pick up the fallen grapes. You will leave them for the poor and the stranger. I am Yahweh your God. You will not steal, nor deal deceitfully or fraudulently with your fellow-citizen. You will not swear by my name with the intent to deceive and thus profane the name of your God. I am Yahweh. You will not exploit or rob your fellow. You will not keep the labourer's wage until next morning . . . You will not harbour hatred for your brother . . . You will not exact vengeance on, or bear any sort of grudge against, the members of your race, but will love your neighbour as yourself. I am Yahweh. (Lev. 19: 9–18)

Jesus picks up where Leviticus leaves off:

And now a lawyer stood up and, to test him, asked, 'Master, what must I do to inherit eternal life?' He said to him, 'What is written in the Law? What is your reading of it?' He replied, 'You must love the Lord your God with all your heart, with all your soul, and with all your strength, and with all your mind, and your neighbour as yourself.' Jesus said to him, 'You have answered right, do this and life is yours.' (Luke 10: 25–28)

But the lawyer wanted to be clever, and he asked our Lord the difficult question 'Who is my neighbour?', receiving the majestic reply that has reverberated through the centuries, namely the story of the good Samaritan. The Jews were undoubtedly aware of the commandment to love one's neighbour, but they interpreted this as a member of one's race. What Jesus did was to enlarge the concept of neighbour to everyone.

But it is in the Johannine gospels and epistles, and the Pauline epistles, that we have the most powerful pronouncements of love. In John's gospel we find:

> This is my commandment:
> love one another,
> as I have loved you.
> No one can have greater love
> than to lay down his life for his friends.
>
> (John 15:12–13)

Paul's epistles are filled with the concept of love and his majestic sayings on the subject reach their apotheosis in his first epistle to the Corinthians:

> Though I command languages both human and angelic – if I speak without love, I am no more than a gong booming or a cymbal clashing. And though I have the power of prophecy, to penetrate all mysteries and knowledge, and though I have all the faith necessary to move mountains – if I am without love, I am nothing. Though I should give away to the poor all that I possess, and even give up my body to be burned – if I am without love, it will do me no good whatever. Love is always patient and kind; love is never jealous; love is not boastful or conceited, it is never rude and never seeks its own advantage, it does not take offence or store up grievances. Love does not rejoice at wrongdoing, but finds its joy in the truth. It is always ready to make allowances, to trust, to hope and to endure whatever comes. Love never comes to an end. (1 Cor. 13: 1–8)

An analysis of the great oration by Paul would clarify the

essential components of personal love, and they will be echoed in various parts of the book.

It is, however, a final return to John, now in his epistle, that gives us the ultimate significance of love:

> My dear friends,
> let us love each other,
> since love is from God
> and everyone who loves is a child of God and knows God.
> Whoever fails to love does not know God,
> because God is love.
>
> (1 John 4: 7–8)

God is love, and love of neighbour is the summation of all Christian teaching. In marriage two people vow to love one another for life, and in the vicissitudes of this love they encounter God in each other by day:

> No one has ever seen God,
> but as long as we love each other
> God remains in us
> and his love comes to its perfection in us.
>
> (1 John 4: 12)

God is the unseen and the unknown force that holds the world together, and in the process each one of us. He does that in and through love. As long as we are loving, then we are in his presence and he is in us. In fact we love many people, but the person we love most constantly is our spouse and every moment is a choice for or against loving him or her. So marriage is the central sacrament of love through which we find God. This does not mean that those who are single, separated, divorced, unloved, cannot find God, or are not in the presence of God – everyone has their way of being in the presence of God – but it does mean that for the married God is to be found continuously in the neighbour of spouse and in the children. In the presence of that love the invisible God becomes visible.

Marital love takes many forms, and it is in this variety that

6

spans increasingly half a century that the modern drama of the spiritual life is lived by the majority of people.

2

Marriage and Sexuality in the Scriptures

Looking through the Scriptures on the topic of marriage and sexuality, we do not find an obvious connection with love. There is some link, but the main motif is the goodness of creation and the relationship of this creation to God.

There is a significant revelation in Genesis which relates the man-woman relationship to God. This vital link receives very little attention in Christian circles. In the first chapter of Genesis we find: 'God said, "Let us make man in our own image, in the likeness of ourselves." ' (v. 26). From this fundamental sentence we find that men and women are created in the image of God, that is, in the light of what we have seen in the previous chapter, they have the capacity to love and to create in and through that love. Just below we find:

> God created man in the image of himself,
> in the image of God he created him,
> male and female he created them.
>
> (Gen. 1:27)

What is so significant in this sentence is that in creating men and women in his image God is shown to be a mystery which contains a sexual dimension of the constituents of maleness and femaleness. The predominantly male description of God has not left much room for Christians to appreciate that sexuality, with all its richness, is of the very essence of the Godhead. Christianity has been so alienated from sexual matters that the idea of sexuality inhabiting the very Godhead has not had much favour. Nevertheless the idea is very much there, and part of Christianity's reappraisal of sexuality is the need to appreciate that men and women reflect a basic characteristic of the divine.

In this first passage of Genesis, God blesses the couple and invites them to be fruitful:

> God blessed them, saying to them 'Be fruitful, multiply, fill the earth and subdue it. Be masters of the fish of the sea, the birds of heaven and all the living creatures that move on earth.' God also said, 'Look, to you I give all the seed-bearing plants everywhere on the surface of the earth, and all the trees with seed-bearing fruit; this will be your food. And to all the wild animals, all the birds of heaven and all the living creatures that creep along the ground, I give all the foliage of the plants as their food.' And so it was. God saw all he had made, and indeed it was very good. (Gen. 1:28–31)

The key words here are that the creation of men and women with the distinct blessing of fruitfulness was very good. God rejoices in the man-woman relationship that leads to new life. Having created the world, God has delegated its continuation to mankind, and we, as viceroys, have the task of continuing the human race through the gift of sexuality. It is a precious gift which in fact determines the whole structure of human relations. Christianity needs to appreciate that the man-woman encounter is the fundamental unit of sexuality on which the world was built, and to have treated it in a subordinate, disparaging way is a repudiation of a central revelation from God.

It is in the second chapter of Genesis, which is thought to have been written first, that we find the specific man-woman encounter. Here we see the basic orientation of the couple towards each other as the central pillar of God's plan for mankind:

> Yahweh God said, 'It is not right that the man should be alone. I shall make him a helper.' . . . Then, Yahweh God made the man fall into a deep sleep. And, while he was

asleep, he took one of his ribs and closed the flesh up again forthwith. Yahweh God fashioned the rib he had taken from the man into a woman, and brought her to the man. And the man said:

> This one at last is bone of my bones
>   and flesh of my flesh!
> She is to be called Woman,
>   because she was taken from Man.

This is why a man leaves his father and mother and becomes attached to his wife, and they become one flesh. Now, both of them were naked, the man and his wife, but they felt no shame before each other. (Gen. 2:18–25)

In this passage the language of marriage is used and the departure from the parental home to set up a new unit is clearly outlined. The essential sexual unity of marriage is spelt out, and we are told that there should be no sense of shame in the encounter.

To sum up these passages, we see that in God's plan for mankind there is a union between a man and a woman, who are of equal worth, which provides the fundamental relationship for the sexes, with which new life can start. Although procreation is clearly a basic construct of the unity of the sexes, it is their relationship with each other that provides the fundamental background.

MARRIAGE AND COVENANT

Israel was a nation whose people had a covenant with Yahweh their God. God promised his divine approval and guaranteed his support in exchange for obedience to his laws. Thus a special alliance was created between God and his people who became his favourites. The covenant was a crucial concept in the Jewish faith because it marked an undeserved gift to Israel who became special and had a unique relationship with its God. This covenant was portrayed in a variety of ways, of which marriage was a particular symbol.

But the covenant was subject to stress and strain. The Jewish people were subject to disobedience and unfaithfulness, and regularly tested God's patience and love. This conflictual relationship is depicted in the marriage of the prophet Hosea whose wife was unfaithful to him. He writes of his anger towards her, and then his forgiveness and reconciliation in the same way that Yahweh was angry with unfaithful Israel and yet forgave and was reconciled with her.

Here we find Hosea raging against his wife/Israel:

To court, take your mother to court!
For she is no longer my wife
nor am I her husband.
She must either remove her whoring ways from her face
and her adulteries from between her breasts,
or I shall strip her and expose her
naked as the day she was born;
I will make her as bare as the desert,
I shall make her as dry as arid country,
and let her die of thirst.
And I shall feel no pity for her children
since they are the children of her whorings.
Yes, their mother has played the whore,
she who conceived them has disgraced herself
by saying, 'I shall chase after my lovers;
they will assure me my keep,
my wool, my flax, my oil and my drinks.

(Hos. 2:4–7)

But his wife, Israel, repents and wants to be reconciled to her husband/Yahweh:

But look, I am going to seduce her
and lead her into the desert
and speak to her heart.
There I shall give her back her vineyards,
and make the Vale of Achor a gateway of hope.

11

> There she will respond as when she was young,
> As on the day when she came up from Egypt

(a clear suggestion of Yahweh's salvific intervention in saving the Jewish people in their exodus from Egypt).

> When that day comes – declares Yahweh –
> You will call me, 'My husband',
> No more will you call me 'My Baal'

(a foreign God worshipped by Israel when she was unfaithful to Yahweh).

> I shall banish the names of the Baals from her lips
> and their name will be mentioned no more.
> When that day comes I shall make a treaty for them with the
> wild animals . . .
> I shall betroth you to myself for ever,
> I shall betroth you in uprightness and justice,
> and faithful love and tenderness.
>
> (Hos. 2:14–21)

The covenant, the special relationship between Yahweh is represented beautifully in this marriage story of unfaithfulness and reconciliation. This interaction between faith and marriage is a sign of the secular reality of marriage being taken up and made into a divine mystery. In the following paragraph the story is abbreviated: 'Yahweh said to me, "Go again, love a woman who loves another man, an adulteress, and love her as Yahweh loves the Israelites although they turn to other gods and love raisin cakes" ' (Hos. 3:1).

CHRIST AND THE CHURCH

This intimate link between God and marriage is continued in the New Testament in Paul's epistle to the Ephesians.

The setting of Paul's teaching is the subordinate role of women which prevailed at the time, but despite this there is

12

a breakthrough in his understanding that marriage is about love and intimacy which is the way that Christ relates to his church. Paul's letter captures the inner world of marriage as an expression of the divine. In the Old Testament it is the covenant, the relationship between Yahweh and his people which marriage symbolises; in Paul it is the relationship between Christ and his church.

> Be subject to one another out of reverence for Christ. Wives should be subject to their husbands as to the Lord, since, as Christ is head of the Church and saves the whole body, so is a husband the head of his wife; and as the Church is subject to Christ, so should wives be to their husbands, in everything. Husbands should love their wives, just as Christ loved the Church and sacrificed himself for her to make her holy by washing her in cleansing water with a form of words, so that when he took the Church to himself she would be glorious, with no speck or wrinkle or anything like that, but holy and faultless. In the same way, husbands must love their wives as they love their own bodies, for a man to love his wife is for him to love himself. A man never hates his own body, but he feeds it and looks after it; and that is the way Christ treats the Church, because we are parts of his Body. This is why a man leaves his father and mother and becomes attached to his wife, and the two become one flesh. This mystery has great significance, but I am applying it to Christ and the Church. To sum up: you also, each one of you, must love his wife as he loves himself, and let every wife respect her husband. (Eph. 5:21–33)

The concept of the wife respecting her husband sounds awkward in our present age of egalitarian relationships between the sexes, and reflects no more than the prevailing social ethos of the first century AD. But what is remarkable in this passage is how Paul captures the husband-wife unity in and through love as the equivalent of the link between Christ and the Church, and plunges marriage into the very depths of the divine love.

13

SEXUALITY

We know that sexuality has had a rough ride since the early inception of Christianity, but its roots in the Scriptures are solidly based. We have already seen in the second chapter of Genesis the clear indication that a man leaves his father and mother and becomes attached to his wife and the two become one flesh. Furthermore the prelude to sexual intercourse, namely nakedness, was not associated with any sense of shame.

It is, however, to the Song of Songs that we turn for a remarkable and positive evaluation of erotic beauty. Included in the Bible is this remarkable piece of writing in which a couple express in poetic language the fact that they enjoy each other's bodies. The couple are clearly in love with each other, and the passionate love of our day is anticipated some three thousand years ago. This is how the man exclaimed his feelings for his beloved:

> How beautiful you are, my beloved,
> how beautiful you are!
> Your eyes are doves,
> behind your veil;
> your hair is like a flock of goats
> surging down Mount Gilead.
> Your teeth, a flock of sheep to be shorn,
> when they come up from the washing.
> Each one has its twin,
> not one unpaired with another.
> Your lips are a scarlet thread
> and your words enchanting.
> Your cheeks, behind your veil,
> are halves of pomegranate.
> Your neck is the Tower of David
> built on layers,
> hung round with a thousand bucklers,
> and each the shield of a hero.
> Your two breasts are two fawns,

twins of a gazelle,
that feed among the lilies.

(S. of S. 4:1–5)

And this is the response of the woman, the beloved:

My love is fresh and ruddy
to be known among ten thousand.
His head is golden, purest gold,
his locks are palm fronds
and black as the raven.
His eyes are like doves
beside the water courses,
bathing themselves in milk,
perching on a fountain-rim.
His cheeks are beds of spices,
Banks sweetly scented.
His lips are lilies,
distilling pure myrrh.
His hands are golden, rounded,
set with jewels of Tarshish.
His belly a block of ivory
covered with sapphires.
His legs are alabaster columns
set in sockets of pure gold.
His appearance is that of Lebanon,
unrivalled as the cedars.
His conversation is sweetness itself,
he is altogether loveable.
Such is my love, such is my friend,
O daughters of Jerusalem.

(S. of S. 5: 10–16)

In these and similar passages of the Song of Songs we have
the apotheosis of erotic love situated in a biblical setting, and
no amount of disapproval can deny the wonder of God's gift
in human sexuality.

There are, however, warnings against the allure of female
beauty. In Ecclesiasticus we find:

15

> Do not be taken in by a woman's beauty,
> never lose your head over a woman.
>
> (Ecclus 25:21)

And there are a number of clear-cut diatribes against women: 'No spite can approach the spite of a woman' (Ecclus 25: 19); and these include the dangers of irresponsible sexual allure:

> A woman's wantonness shows in her wide-eyed look,
> her eyelashes have no doubt.
> Keep a headstrong daughter under firm control,
> or, feeling free, she will take advantage of it.
> Keep a strict watch on her shameless eye,
> Do not be surprised if she disgraces you.
> Like a thirsty traveller she will open her mouth
> And drink any water she comes across;
> She will sit down in front of every tent-peg
> And open her quiver to every arrow.
>
> (Ecclus 26:9–12)

But there is a handy reminder of the value of a good wife:

> How blessed is the husband of a really good wife;
> the number of his days will be doubled.
> A perfect wife is the joy of her husband,
> he will live out the years of his life in peace.
> A good wife is the best of portions,
> reserved for those who fear the Lord;
> rich or poor, their hearts will be glad,
> their faces cheerful, whatever the season.
>
> (Ecclus 26:1–4)

JESUS AND MARRIAGE

To the best of our knowledge, Jesus never married. At the end of the chapter consideration will be given to the implications of his single state, but short of marriage he did and said a number of significant things on its behalf.

16

He opened his public miracles at the wedding feast of Cana where he transformed water into wine for the couple who were marrying and their family. He must have approved of marriage if he associated it with such an intervention. He not only approved of marriage, but also safeguarded it by insisting on its permanency and against divorce. When he was challenged over the latter issue he replied unequivocally:

Some Pharisees approached him and asked, 'Is it lawful for a man to divorce his wife?' They were putting him to the test. He answered them, 'What did Moses command you?' They replied, 'Moses allowed us to draw up a writ of dismissal in cases of divorce.' Then Jesus said to them, 'It was because you were so hard-hearted that he wrote this commandment for you. But from the beginning of creation he made them male and female. This is why a man leaves his father and mother, and the two become one flesh. They are no longer two, therefore, but one flesh. So then, what God has united, human beings must not divide.' Back in the house the disciples questioned him again about this, and he said to them, 'Whoever divorces his wife and marries another is guilty of adultery against her. And if a woman divorces her husband and marries another she is guilty of adultery too.' (Mark 10:2–12)

At a stroke Jesus changed the lax law of divorce prevailing in Israel to a firm one in favour of marriage, which the Church in the West has maintained until our own day. Unfortunately this firmness has only prevailed in the teaching of the churches and very little has been done to support marriage in these changing and testing times (see Chapter 21).

The third feature of Jesus' distinctive approach was his relationship to women. In his day women were considered to be subordinate to men, and their role confined to the home. Jesus took a very different attitude. He shared his meals with them in the case of Mary and Martha; and on other occasions he revealed his identity to the Samaritan woman at the well, he healed the woman afflicted with the loss of blood, and he forgave the prostitute. Placing women in such a high profile was quite unusual for his age, and his approach heralded the advent of the equality of worth of the sexes which we are trying to achieve in our own day.

This respect for women is shown in the fact that he demands a much higher degree of sexual chastity. He knows that men are capable of adultery, that is, of becoming involved sexually with a woman without any care, concern or love for her; just treating her as an object of lust. Jesus directs his attention not only to the outward behaviour of adultery, which is forbidden, but also to the inner desires of men hidden from the eye: 'You must have heard how it was said, You shall not commit adultery. But I say this to you, if a man looks at a woman lustfully, he has already committed adultery with her in his heart' (Matt. 5:27).

Jesus set standards of sexual integrity which were unbelievably hard because He took men and women, particularly the latter, very seriously. They reflected the image of God, and he directed our attention to perfection, in and through love. In loving our neighbour we love God. These high standards contrast with the deliberate exhibition of naked and half-naked women in our time as the means of selling all forms of goods, and in this way making women appear as objects.

JESUS AND HIS FAMILY

Although Jesus places marriage and the family in the very midst of God's plan for mankind, he distanced himself from his own family.

Right from the earliest stage of his development, we see Jesus taking an independent course from his parents. At the age of twelve when he was returning from Jerusalem where he and his parents had celebrated the feast of Passover, he hid himself in the Temple:

It happened that, three days later, they found him in the Temple, sitting among the teachers, listening to them, and asking them questions; and all those who heard him were astounded at his intelligence and his replies. They were

18

overcome when they saw him, and his mother said to him, 'My child, why have you done this to us? See how worried your father and I have been, looking for you.' He replied, 'Why were you looking for me? Did you not know that I must be in my Father's house?' But they did not understand what he meant. (Luke 2:46–50)

At this early stage we see Jesus separating himself from his earthly parents to become closely identified with his heavenly Father. He was giving them advance warning that he was destined for different things from those they expected of him, although his mother must have increasingly pondered the unusual events associated with her son.

His relatives became disturbed at the way that Jesus conducted himself, particularly as the crowds which followed him became increasingly bigger: 'He went home again, and once more such a crowd collected that they could not even have a meal. When his relations heard of this, they set out to take charge of him; they said, "He is out of his mind" ' (Mark 3:20–21).

To this very day we tend to call people mad when we do not understand their behaviour, which appears bizarre to us. Jesus' relations were no exception. They saw him being increasingly surrounded by people who flocked around him. Close as they were to him, they could not see the extraordinary attraction of his message. They could only see the youngster who grew up in their midst and carried out carpentry as his father had done. For them he was a mere mortal of ordinary proportions. There was nothing outstanding about him in their eyes.

But Jesus had passed on to a new phase of vision. He knew in the depths of his being that God had called him; a God he felt and could call his Father was summoning him to a more important mission. And so he continued to distance himself from his relatives in ways which appeared nothing short of brutal:

Now his mother and his brothers arrived and, standing outside, sent a message, asking for him. A crowd was sitting around him at the time the message was passed to him, 'Look, your mother and brothers and sisters are outside asking for you.' He replied, 'Who are my mother and my brothers?' And looking at those sitting in a circle around him, he said, 'Here are my mother and my brothers. Anyone who does the will of God, that person is my brother and sisters and mother. (Mark 3:31–35)

By now Jesus had totally identified with God, and his earthly family could not be allowed to hinder the work he had to do on behalf of the kingdom of God. God came first, and his relatives distinctly second.

JESUS' SINGLE STATE

Given that Jesus distanced himself from his family, it is not surprising that he did not form a family of his own. The fact that he remained unmarried was unusual. A Jew would normally marry. But Jesus did not, and by remaining single has left the religion he set up bereft of any characteristic Christian model of marriage. In fact the combination of his virgin birth, single state and the preferred state of Paul to be single, has left Christianity a problem of how to present marriage. Although in the Catholic tradition marriage is held to be a sacrament, nevertheless for a long time, and to this very day, the single state dedicated to God is considered to be superior. The single state dedicated to God is not, of course, a sacrament, and in my view marriage as a sacrament must be held to be superior. But this is a matter of argument. What is beyond dispute is that, until recently, married Christians, if not actually apologetic about their state, did not know where precisely to situate it in the order of salvation. Clearly this would not have been the case if Jesus had married.

We do not know why Jesus did not marry, and we shall never know because the Scriptures are silent about it. We have a clue when in the gospel of Mark he states that in heaven there is no marriage (Mark 12:25). Jesus, as the Son of God, belonged to the divine world of relationship in which the Trinity had its own special inner world where marriage does not feature.

But if we leave revelation, let us consider for a moment the implications of a marriage for Jesus. If he had married, he would have had to confine his exclusivity to one woman and the children she bore him. He would have had to restrict himself to a small circle of friends. In other words, he would have had to return to the conditions from which he freed himself from his own relatives. The freedom he exercised in his movements, preaching, and relations, would have been impossible. The man who came to be available to all would have been restricted to a small circle of relatives. Given what he came to mean, as the Son of God, the exclusivity would have been incompatible with his mission. God could not have been narrowed down to one woman and one family. So in my view the authentic Jesus, the Christ, could not have married and still be available to the whole world. But that does not mean that he did not appreciate the importance of marriage for others, and, as we have seen, he started his public miracles at a wedding.

PAUL

Paul may have been married, but at the time of his ministry he is talking as a single person, and he has a predilection for the single state: 'To the unmarried and to widows I say: it is good for them to stay as they are, like me' (1 Cor. 7:8). Later in the epistle he explains why he wants them to stay single:

> I should like you to have your minds free from all worry. The unmarried man gives his mind to the Lord's affairs and to how he can please the Lord; but the man who is married gives his mind to the affairs of this world and to how he can please his wife, and he is divided in mind. (1 Cor. 7:32–34)

And the same applies to the single woman.

21

But Paul is very conscious of sexual desire and the need for a partner:

> Yet to avoid immorality every man should have his own wife and every woman her own husband. The husband must give to his wife what she has a right to expect, and so too the wife to her husband . . . You must not deprive each other, except by mutual consent for a limited time, to leave yourselves free for prayer, and to come together again afterwards. (1 Cor. 7:2–5)

Paul repeats Jesus' teaching on divorce:

> To the married I give this ruling, and this is not mine but the Lord's: a wife must not be separated from her husband – or if she has already left him, she must remain unmarried or else be reconciled to her husband – and a husband must not divorce his wife. (1 Cor. 7:10–11)

Paul is also a strong advocate of chastity:

> Keep away from sexual immorality. All other sins that someone may commit are done outside the body; but the sexually immoral person sins against his own body. Do you not realise that your body is the temple of the Holy Spirit, who is in you and whom you received from God? You are not your own property, then; you have been bought at a price. So use your body for the glory of God. (1 Cor. 6:18–20)

Paul's attitude to women is mixed. On the one hand he sees them as clearly subordinate to men; on the other hand everyone is equal in Jesus: 'There can be neither Jew nor Greek, there can be neither slave nor freeman, there can be neither male nor female – for you are all one in Christ Jesus' (Gal. 3:28).

As already mentioned, Paul places a supreme value on love, and in a typical Pauline way he says further in the epistle to the Galatians:

After all, brothers, you were called to be free; do not use your freedom as an opening for self-indulgence, but be servants to one another in love, since the whole of the Law is summarised in the one commandment: You must love your neighbour as yourself. If you go snapping at one another and tearing one another to pieces, take care: You will be eaten up by one another. (Gal. 5:13–15)

This brief perusal of the Old and the New Testaments testifies to the centrality of sexuality and marriage in this world. It is the way that most people experience intimacy and love which leads to fruitfulness and joint responsibility for children. The body, which Christ took on in the incarnation, is the instrument of love through which we continue the race, and in the process put into practice, each successive generation, the fruits of love. God has given us this world to explore and each other to love, and the central way we do this is in an intimate relationship of personal love.

3

Contemporary Marriage

In the preface it is stated that marriage will be considered as a secular reality taken up in the Lord and made into a divine mystery. What is meant by this is that there is no fixed given concept of Christian marriage as there is of the Eucharist or baptism. What is clear is that the social reality of marriage changes from age to age, and it is this changing institution which is considered to be holy, indeed has been treated by the Roman Catholic Church for the last thousand years as a sacrament. But whether we consider marriage, in the Christian sense, as a holy estate, or as a sacrament, it is clear that within it God is present. God, however, is present in an ever-changing social entity. Provided this social entity is a permanent, exclusive, monogamous, and a faithful relationship, then it is Christian marriage, but in order to understand Christian marriage at any time we have to appreciate its inner social and psychological world which is constantly evolving.

In this chapter we shall look briefly at how the secular and religious reality has changed in the last 150 years. During this time the principal concern of the couple has been the birth and raising of their children, and society has become more aware of the needs of children. Offspring became less and less objects of financial support for their parents. Acts of Parliament have meant that slowly universal education became the object of society's preoccupation with children. As poverty and ill-health receded, infant mortality became reduced and children increasingly survived pregnancy, birth and the early years of life. In the upper social strata, children were kept within the family, and no longer sent out to be educated in other homes.

This advance in status for children has become coupled with increased duration of life. Men and women live longer and, in the period we are considering, some twenty to twenty-five years have been added on average to life's expectation. This means that couples have two or three further decades beyond the child-bearing period and marriage, which starts as a dyad, returns to a dyad after the children have left home. So the life of the couple is assuming a dimension well beyond the procreation and rearing of children. It is this growing emphasis on the personal and interpersonal quality of the life of the couple that has engaged so much interest, particularly in the past fifty years.

At the same time as both children and couples survive for longer periods, society has increasingly taken over from parents tasks which were exclusively the concern of the parents and the family. Mention has already been made of education. Another feature is health. Shortly after the Second World War ended, the Health Service was introduced in Britain which meant that the care of serious illness could take place in hospital free of charge. Parents were freed of the responsibility for looking after seriously ill children, and when a spouse fell ill their partner could take advantage of the care provided by the hospitals. Coupled with this service were major advances in medical care, so that both adults and children were freed from much infirmity and unnecessary mortality. This released the energies of the couple to orientate them towards each other.

To health and education can be added housing. The increased availability of housing meant that spouses and children could have separate abodes. This gave them independence and privacy, but it also meant later on that the elderly were isolated as the extended family was no longer housed in the same unit.

All this social welfare of housing, education and health was underpinned by social benefits which have varied according to the political climate of the day, but throughout the post-war period there has remained a minimum network of support which has acted as a protection against sheer poverty.

The total effect of these social changes has meant a

liberation from the tasks of survival to the concern of the quality of life, and particularly the private life of the spouses and their children. This period has coincided with an emergence of psychology in all its various dimensions, but particularly the work of Freud and his successors has popularised the world of feelings, emotions and sexuality. Freud's emphasis on sexuality and aggression has meant that these two aspects of life have become immensely important. Once again the focus had shifted to the interpersonal relationships of married people, and an industry has emerged of popular psychology with extensive literature, by which couples judge the quality of their life. As formal religion has receded into the background, men and women are no longer preoccupied with sin, but with the quality of their sex life. Sex clinics have risen which try to respond to the widespread concern for sexual fulfilment. In addition to sex, psychology has stressed the world of feelings and emotions, and the affective life has become as important as the sexual life.

This increasing preoccupation with the inner world of the personal life of the couple has taken place while the roles of the couple themselves have been radically changing. Traditionally, in the industrial setting of towns and cities, the husband had been the wage-earner, and gone out of the home to work and support the family. This financial power gave him superiority in other spheres, rendering him the head of the family, the person who had authority, made decisions, and was its ambassador to the outside world. The wife stayed at home, and her role was considered to be that of child provider, child rearer and basically the housekeeper.

Within the short period of the last thirty years, these traditional roles are changing. Woman's emancipation has been most influential, coupled with the fact that they are as well-educated and trained as men. Increasingly women go out to work, and have as much economic power as the men. Decisions are no longer taken unilaterally, and responsibility for running the home has become a shared experience.

Thus in a very short time couples have become infinitely more egalitarian, far more materially secure, and have much less of their energy taken up with reproduction as the size of the family is reduced to two or less children, and the timing is accurately pinpointed with efficient contraception. Indeed widespread contraception, the result of scientific advances of the last thirty years, means that the overwhelming amount of sexual activity within marriage is non-procreative. Contraception is, of course, a mixed blessing because, with the fear of pregnancy removed, there is little to oppose pre- and extra-marital sex.

We can sum up the changes of the last hundred and fifty years, but particularly in this century, as a reduction of social responsibilities of the couple, with increasing independence and privacy, in which the quality of personal life has become increasingly important. Thus private life is tending to emphasise feelings and sexuality, and spouses are increasingly concerned with a relationship that is built on love, and strives to live on love. Couples are no longer struggling to survive physically and emotionally, but are free to be good friends. Thus contemporary marriage has become an intimate relationship of love which has to be maintained for forty or fifty years. This is the secular reality on which Christian marriage has to be built.

CHRISTIAN DIMENSION

At the same time as the secular reality has been changing, in the last thirty years there have been major attempts to reconsider Christian marriage in the Second Vatican Council in the Catholic Church, and in two reports in the Anglican Church called *Marriage, Divorce and the Church* and *Marriage and the Church's Task*, and in documents of other churches.

As far as the Roman Catholic Church is concerned, its description of marriage until the Second Vatican Council was highly legal and consisted of definitions which had been inherited from the Middle Ages. They described marriage in terms of ends. The primary end was the procreation and education of children, and the secondary end the 'mutual help' of the spouses and the relief of concupiscence. Both the language and the concepts of the ends were increasingly

27

criticised in the thirties and forties, and there was much rebuttal of these criticisms. Nevertheless at the Second Vatican Council both the language and the legal, canonical basis of marriage were dropped. For those who see the Roman Catholic Church as a monolithic, unchanging institution they need to read the treatment of marriage within that Church in the last fifty years. They will be amazed at the changes that have occurred.

The language of primary and secondary ends has disappeared and the basis of marriage has now become love:

> The wellbeing of the individual person and of human and Christian society is intimately linked with the healthy condition of that community produced by marriage and family. Hence Christians and all men who hold this community in high esteem sincerely rejoice in the various ways by which men today find help in fostering this community of love. (Pastoral Constitution, Part 2, ch. 1)

Marriage and the family are now considered a community of love:

> The biblical Word of God several times urges the betrothed and the married to nourish and develop their wedlock by pure conjugal love and undivided affection. Many men of our new age also highly regard true love between husband and wife as it manifests itself in a variety of ways depending on the worthy customs of various peoples and times. This love is an eminently human one since it is directed from one person to another through an affection of the will. It involves the good of the whole person . . . This love the Lord has judged worthy of special gifts, healing, perfecting, and exalting gifts of grace and of charity. (ibid.)

The unique importance of the family lived as a community of love is that it manifests Christ as God who is love in the world:

> Thus the Christian family, which springs from marriage as

28

a reflection of the loving covenant uniting Christ and the Church, and as a participation in that covenant, will manifest to all men the Saviour's living presence in the world, and the genuine nature of the Church. This the family will do by the mutual love of the spouses, by their generous fruitfulness, their solidarity and faithfulness, and by the loving way in which all members of the family work together. (ibid.)

In these few passages the Roman Catholic Church placed marriage squarely in the realm of personal love, and strongly influenced by its biblical tradition, sees the love as portraying Christ's love and ultimately the foundation of our faith. Thus human love becomes the means of exploring divine love.

The Anglican Church produced two reports on marriage. I quote from the second, *Marriage and the Church's Task*:

[Marriage] is a relational bond of personal love, a compound of commitment, experience and response, in which the commitment clothes itself in the flesh and blood of a living union. The commitment looks forward to this deeper union of love . . . The commitment is made in love and for love. (Section 99)

In this statement the Anglican Church independently affirms that marriage is constituted of a lifelong commitment which is immersed in love:

Marriage is a relationship of shared commitment and love. It is a commitment in which nothing is deliberately withheld. As such, it is a profound sharing of present experience. As such, it also anticipates the sharing of future experience. It is a commitment through time. It embraces the future as well as the present. It intends and promises permanence.

The logic of such intention and promise is as follows. Love in marriage not only unites two persons as they are, it also recreates them as they shall become. It is 'person making'. (Sections 87 and 88)

Both the Catholic and the Anglican statements lead on from this personal to sexual love.

In the Second Vatican Council text we find:

This love is uniquely expressed and perfected through the marital act. The actions within marriage by which the couple are united intimately and chastely are noble and worthy ones. Expressed in a manner which is truly human, these actions signify and promote the mutual self-giving by which spouses enrich each other with a joyful and thankful will. (Pastoral Constitution, Part 2, ch. 1)

In the Anglican statement we find:

This polyphony of love finds expression in the lovers' bodily union. This is not to be comprehended simply in terms of two individuals' experience of ecstatic pleasure. Such it certainly may be; but it is always more. It is an act of personal commitment which spans past, present and future. It is celebration, healing, renewal, pledge and promise. Sexual intercourse can 'mean' many different things to husband and wife, according to mood and circumstance. Above all, it communicates the affirmation of mutual belonging. (Section 89)

CONVERGENCE

It can be thus seen that both the secular and the theological are converging in our own day to the concept of marriage and the family as a community of love. For me, this is the greatest opportunity of bringing the two together and examining how they can interact. Love needs continuity, reliability and predictability, which are to be found in the concept of permanence which since Jesus's time has been the model of Christian marriage. Permanence allows 'two persons to be joined together in a new duality-in-unity and discover a new freedom in interdependence'. This permanence, however, is

30

not to be interpreted as a static stability. The world of the partners is dynamic, and their love is a bubbling cauldron of energy.

Unfortunately the modern couple have been thrown into this world of love which neither society nor the Church understands too well. The result has been high rates of divorce throughout western society as couples struggle to understand and live with the concept of loving intimacy. The challenge is to understand the meaning of love so that it can be lived for fifty years without the need to change partners. This book is dedicated to this task, and we begin with asking the question in the next chapter, 'What is love?'

4

What is Love?

There is no agreed definition of what love is. Is it the thrill of the chase? Is it the excitement of being in close proximity to the beloved? Is it the connections with sex and sexual intercourse? Or is it the moment-to-moment pleasure of being involved with, sharing and doing things for someone who matters? Each of these moments can be exciting. In this chapter an evolutionary view of love is presented, that is, that acts of love exist because they serve in the generation of the offspring who will in turn reproduce themselves, thus keeping humanity going.

In order to have children we need to find a mate, and the first process of love concerns sexual attraction. Men and women have different needs when it comes to sexual attraction. Men seek attractive women who have the quality of beauty, age and health. This is all bound up with eroticism. Traditionally Christianity has been frightened of the erotic, but in an evolutionary sense it is the background that supplies the energy to the subsequent union. Men seek beautiful women. Women are also attracted by male beauty, but even more important they need male qualities that ensure security for the subsequent needs of the child. Thus women would be influenced by evidence of money, possessions, status, ambition and industry. The evolutionary model thus encourages female attractiveness and male stability which will encourage sexual intercourse and fertilisation and provision for the helpless infant. In fact while these qualities are influential, the final choice requires social and psychological aptness in addition to erotic and material suitability. A good marriage needs more than beauty and money. Couples have to retain the interest of each other, other than in land and the maintenance of a home. They have to stimulate, encourage, support, excite and fire each other's imagination, but the base design is of perpetual attraction and social stability.

Having obtained a partner, the next requirement of the evolutionary model is for exclusivity. Exclusivity is another word for ensuring that the couple raise their own children and remain available for their nurturing. The two threats to exclusivity are infidelity and the disappearance of a spouse. The infidelity of a wife endangers her to a pregnancy, and the risk that the husband will be asked to raise someone else's children. Even the occasional act of infidelity on the part of a woman used to risk a pregnancy in the days before effective contraceptives; hence the long and universal importance of fidelity. Male infidelity meant that he could fertilise another woman, and redirect resources from his own family to the raising of other children. Fidelity nowadays is important because in the prevailing intimacy of the couple infidelity is an act of disloyalty and betrayal which undermines trust.

The next factor is the preservation of the spouses to ensure the nurturing of the children. In the past death was the single most important danger to parental presence. Nowadays marital breakdown and divorce have replaced the most common reason for parental departure.

Most societies have developed cultural institutions to safeguard fidelity and the presence of spouses, of which the most common is marriage.

Thus the selection of a partner and the subsequent exclusive relationship within marriage form the background to love. Within marriage erotic attraction leads to sexual intercourse for the purposes of procreation. When infant mortality was high and the duration of life short, sexual intercourse was largely, or almost exclusively, concerned with procreation. Nowadays with advances in medicine, the reduction of family size, the advent of contraception, the majority of sexual intercourse is non-reproductive and is channelled towards the strengthening of the bond of the couple. The intense excitation of erotic arousal and sexual pleasure tend to concentrate and associate love with sexual activity. In the evolutionary model the erotic component is primarily at the service of fertilisation, the meeting of ovum and sperm.

Once children are produced they must be fed, nurtured, protected, taught and loved. This is the final consequence of the evolutionary model. The love of parents for their children which evokes acts of intense heroism and the quiet and persistent efforts over two decades by parents to give their children their best.

The love required by the parents to stay together to nurture their children and the consequent parental love are the least obtrusive but most powerful tokens of love. At the heart of this aspect of love is staying in relationship, and it reflects the divine characteristic of the Trinitarian ability to stay in a loving relationship for eternity.

In this model of evolutionary understanding of love, there are six broad goals. These are display or attractiveness, exclusivity, commitment, marriage, sexual intimacy, reproduction and parenting. The evolutionary approach to love suggests that love acts have evolved to serve these goals because of their consequences of reproductive success. What is needed, however, is an understanding of how mate selection is achieved – what is the mechanism by which two people become bonded to each other?

Still situated within the evolutionary model we have the work of John Bowlby which has thrown light on infant attachment. His work is based on ethology, and he has shown that infants become attached to their mother within a few days to weeks from the time of their birth. This attachment is based on vision, sound, touch and smell. The baby, first in a limited way and then increasingly more strongly, recognises visually first the face and then other parts of the mother's body. Her voice becomes a familiar sound and, of course, the sensations of touch give the baby a sense of security. Through these physical means and the sense of smell, the baby forms an affective attachment, that is to say, it is emotionally bonded to the mother and thereafter wants to stay by her side. If the young child wakes up and finds mother missing, or indeed, mother is absent for any reason, her physical disappearance leads to a sequence of behaviour. First, there is protest which involves crying, and this is followed by searching which can go on for days. If the search is fruitless, it leads to despair, a state of passivity and sadness. Finally there is detachment, in which the bond is broken, and, if the mother returns say after a long period, the baby ignores her. This sequence can also be seen when we lose touch with someone we love, and it is the pattern of loss for any reason.

Bowlby suggests that attachment behaviour characterises human behaviour from cradle to the grave. It is particularly pertinent to that stage of falling in love whereby a particular man or woman becomes the exclusive object of our love. There is a lot of comparison between the attachment of the infant (AI) and a lovers' attachment (LA).

Both (AI) and (LA) are reciprocal. The mother responds to her baby's needs, and lovers are mutually aware of each other. This reciprocity causes the baby and lovers to feel safe, confident and secure. When the mother or lover is not available, then the infant and the lover become anxious, pre-occupied, unable to concentrate. The infant and mother spend a good deal of time holding, touching, caressing, kissing, smiling, clinging to each other, and so do lovers. When infant and lovers are sick, worried, threatened in any respect, they like to be held and soothed by mother and their friend. Both experience distress at separation, searching for the missing mother or lover, and finding no peace until there is a reunion. When reunion takes place, there is intense joy. Although the baby can be attached to more than one person, such as grandmother, nanny, relative, there is usually one key person, normally the mother. Lovers have other friends, but they love one special person who exhibits feelings of jealousy when attention is diverted from them. There is a great deal of non-verbal communication between mother and baby, and also primitive verbal sounds of cooing. Lovers also coo, talk baby language, and use non-verbal communication. This simple but highly effective communication is coupled with an intense awareness of the infants' inner world by the mother. Lovers show the same degree of mutual awareness of each other's inner world, called empathy.

In further work on Bowlby's theories, it has been shown

that the attachment of infants can be divided into three categories, secure, anxious and avoidant. As far as the secure infant is concerned, it believes and acts as if the mother is accessible to him, even when she is out of sight, whereas the anxious baby cries more than the secure baby, clings to her more and cannot use her as a safe base from which to explore their environment. The avoidant baby tries to escape the gaze, contact and intimacy of mother.

Research has shown that these three types of attachment can be found in adults.

In the secure attachment, it is relatively easy to get close to others as well as feeling comfortable depending on them, and in turn being depended upon. Such a person rarely feels the threat of being abandoned. The anxious attachment wants people to be very close, almost to merge with their partner, coupled with the fear that they are not loved or they are not wanted. The avoidant attachment is the one in which the person feels uncomfortable being close to others and finds it difficult to trust them and be dependent on them, or allow them to get too close. It has been found that secure attachment forms about 50 per cent of all attachments, anxious about 25 per cent, and avoidant about 25 per cent.

This description of these three attachment types are associated with certain personality features. Secure people consider themselves as easy to get to know, and as liked by most people, and feel that other people are generally well intentioned and goodhearted. Anxious people indicate they have more self-doubts, are misunderstood and underappreciated, and they trust others less. The avoidant falls between these two categories.

Attachment theory shows that we are equipped genetically to form attachments from the time we are born till the time we die. This ability allows us to form an exclusive relationship with a man or a woman, and enter into the intimate partnership of marriage. It does not tell us, of course, why we choose a particular person, but, when we do make a choice, our behaviour becomes intimate and passionate.

When a choice has been made, a warmth is established within that couple which is expressed in intimacy. Ten signs

36

of intimacy have been identified. They are desiring to promote the welfare of the loved one, experiencing happiness with them, having high regard for them, being able to count on them at times of need, having a mutual understanding, sharing oneself and possessions, receiving emotional support from the loved one, giving mutual support, having intimate communication and valuing them in one's life.

Within the context of this intimacy, passion is expressed in terms of romance, physical attraction and sexual consummation. In most instances sexuality is the main component of passion, but other needs, such as self-esteem, dominance over others, submission and self-actualisation, may be prominent features.

In this chapter an attempt has been made to portray love on a scientific basis from an evolutionary design. The foundations of love are the attraction necessary to bring men and women together to mate and maintain the race. The particular mechanism of attachment forms the specific basis of bonding within the overall evolutionary force. Attachment brings a couple together, and intimacy and passion maintain the attachment.

Disorders of love emerge from this outline when the human acts which lead to attraction and courtship are separated from commitment, leading to casual relationships or, after commitment, to infidelity. Within the orbit of attachment, it can be seen that anxious and avoidant personalities have difficulties with their intimacy requirements, needing in turn too much or too little from their partners.

This group of disorders does not exhaust, by any means, the various forms of the distortions of love, but it gives an outline of how to examine difficulties associated with love.

In the next chapter we shall examine love from a different standpoint, namely the experience we all have as children.*

*This chapter is based on some of the work contained in *The Psychology of Love*, ed. R. L. Sternberg and L. Barnes, Yale University Press, 1988.

5

Childhood Experiences of Love

For nearly everyone the first experiences of love are associated with childhood. As we grow up and consider adult patterns of behaviour as the norm, we tend to ignore our childhood. In fact we spend a great deal of effort to make sure that we are not seen to behave in childish ways. Thus we try to control the impulse of wanting immediate gratification, and we cope with pain and adversity without wanting to run to the nearest comforting figure. What we forget is that the foundations of love are learned in our childhood, and it is to these that we revert when we relax in the intimacy of loving relationships. So in order to understand the nature of our loving expectations we have to understand these deep layers of our childhood experiences.

ATTACHMENT

As already mentioned in the previous chapter, the first critical step of expressing love is effected when we form an affective attachment to our mother in the first few weeks of life. We do this through vision, sound, touch and smell. We begin to recognise slowly first her face, with its various features, and then the rest of the body. We learn to respond to her smiles and frowns, and in this way get the first glimpse of approval and disapproval. The same thing happens with her voice. We become attuned to its various inflexions, from affirmation to severity. The voice gives information about her whereabouts in her physical presence and it forms a radar system of communication with her. It is a means of constant reassurance when she cannot be seen. The most powerful stimulus, however, comes from touch. Holding and being held signal strong affectionate sensations in which the baby feels safe and very much wanted and appreciated. This is also the way to obtain comfort when distress is experienced in the form of physical pain or any form of anxiety. In the depths of the arms of mother we are thus fed both physically and emotionally.

This affective bonding is first experienced with mother, and then in time with father, brother, sister, granny and grandfather. The attachment forms a protective network for the young child, and it gives all of us our first experience of love. If one observes the interaction between a mother or father and their child, there is a reciprocal rhythm of bodily contact, smiling and talking to each other. Thus the foundations of love are laid down in the context of bodily encounter, a feature to which adults will return throughout their life in their loving moments, emotionally and sexually. Whenever we fall in love or make a deep friendship, we form an affective attachment. We are attracted by another's appearance, the sound of their voice, and we want to be in their physical presence and hold them. Thus attachment, as we have seen, is basic to loving, and when we lose the people we love we are sad, cry, and mourn their departure, just as the child cries at the absence of the key figures in its life.

TRUST

Within the physical bonding just described, the child learns the rudiments of trust. Trust is experienced physically, emotionally and intellectually. Physical trust is conveyed through feeling safe and comfortable in the presence of the key attachment figure. This safety and comfort are experienced by a relaxed sensation in the presence of the other person, or when we are held by them. The security continues throughout life, and is felt when we are in the presence of people we recognise as friendly or close to us. Children are totally dependent on their parents and adults for safety; hence the revulsion that is felt when they are physically, emotionally or sexually abused.

As we grow older the signals of trust are conveyed emotionally. We receive messages of trust by the way people smile approvingly, greet or affirm us. All these signals give us the feeling of being surely wanted and approved, and they become the basis for our interaction with other people. These signals test the atmosphere of trust between people.

As we grow older we emerge from the immediacy of physicality and emotionality to cognitive communication. As we begin to understand language and deal in it, trustworthiness is expressed in veracity. We need to believe what people say to us, and in turn they need to believe in us. Hence the importance of the truth. That is why it is so important that we treat our children with the greatest care in respect of the truth. Very soon, by the age of three, they will develop sharp memories and insights into what we have told them, and they will remind us without the slightest hesitation when we contradict ourselves.

One cannot exaggerate the importance of trust in all human affairs, but in particular in loving intimacy. In the latter situation we are offering our bodies, minds and hearts to another person. We need to be able to trust them as completely as possible. In sexual intercourse we reveal our naked bodies which become the instruments of loving mutuality. In conversation we express our deepest thoughts, the truths we have reached by hard work, and we wish them to be treated with care and respect even if people do not agree with them. In our loving exchange we bestow our deepest investment of affection to another and we desire an equivalent reciprocity. It is essential for intimacy that we trust the people closest to us to be reliable. It is this reliability that gives us the basis of trust in the rest of our lives.

AUTONOMY

Within the context of this secure trust, the young child begins to separate from mother and father. Initially it will crawl a few yards away, and then return to the safety of mother's presence. This behaviour has been compared to a ball, to which an elastic has been attached. The elastic is the child which stretches itself for increasingly longer distances, and then flies back to the ball. As it crawls away from the mother, it can let her out of sight for increasingly longer periods, returning to her only when it is frightened, hurt, or a stranger arrives. Thus the child learns to explore its surroundings and to discover new things for itself.

Slowly the child acquires the skill to walk, dress, feed itself and talk. In all these respects it is acquiring its autonomy. This is the first stage in life when we learn the balance between closeness and separateness. For increasingly longer periods, the child will cope by itself, playing on its own or with other children, away from the key parental figure, and then it will return to base, to mother, father, granny, or whoever is its principal attachment figure. In psychological terms it is learning to internalise mother, that is to say, to keep her presence alive inside, in her physical absence.

The same thing applies to adult friendship or love. We spend a lot of our time with the person we love, but we also have to spend time apart. When we are together with those we love we feel a great deal of pleasure. The degree of distress we experience in their absence depends on how much they matter to us and how well we have internalised them. When they feel safe inside us and we have access to them, we can be separate from them for long periods without worry. Some people find it very difficult to let those they love out of their sight. When the beloved is not available they become anxious and frightened. These people do whatever they can to keep their spouse near them. They are called possessive or jealous. Jealousy is the fear of losing someone we love, and it goes back to the child's fear of losing its key attachment figure, which is usually the mother. But most people find a balance between closeness and separateness, and this reflects the reliable presence of parental figures in the early years of life.

CONFLICT

The growing autonomy of the child leads to independent activity. It wants to explore its surroundings, it touches and amuses itself with things it should not. These are moments which lead to frustration, which is associated with anger. Anger and love are closely linked. They are the opposite sides of the same coin. Some psychologists located the roots of frustration and anger in the first few months of life, but it is usually in the second and third year, the time of the beginning of autonomy, that anger is seen most clearly. The child wants to do or handle things its own way, the mother says 'no', and there is conflict. If the child persists, the parent shouts or even smacks, and temporarily there is a rupture of the relationship. After a few seconds or moments, there is reconciliation, forgiveness and reparation.

As adults we also say and do things which hurt those we love, and feel guilty. After a little while we forgive, or are forgiven, we make amends, and the relationship is restored.

In adult relationships we find people who do not negotiate conflict so smoothly. When they hurt someone, they cannot accept responsibility for their behaviour. They blame everyone else except themselves. Another pattern is the person who finds it impossible to apologise. When they have done something wrong, they withdraw into themselves and refuse to be reached. This is called sulking, and some men and women will sulk for hours, and even days. In all these instances reconciliation is hard to achieve.

SELF-ESTEEM

Slowly the growing child is building its self-esteem, that is, love of itself. Self esteem is realised through the child feeling that its sensations, actions, thoughts and feelings are experienced as good. This leads to a basic self-acceptance of itself. Through this self-acceptance it trusts itself and it feels lovable.

Self-esteem is based on the constant affirmation the child receives from its parents and others. Through them it feels that it is good. This goodness is transmitted unconditionally on the basis that the child is present and it exists. It does not have to do anything to merit the approval it receives. It is simply lovable because it is there. The way it experiences this lovability is by feeling recognised, wanted and appreciated.

Self-esteem plays a vital role in human relationships. If we feel lovable, then we allow people to get close, and to love us. We are not afraid of what they will discover when they approach us. We have nothing to hide. Those who are full of self-esteem have a basic goodness at the centre of their personality. They do not need to put on extra external decoration in appearance or status. They present themselves as they are, and expect to be appreciated as such. Those who are unsure of themselves seek to boost their self-esteem by additional embellishment. Equally those who are full of self-esteem feel that they have something of value to offer to others. Their most precious gift is their self, and they do not hesitate to donate themselves fully. The Last Supper was such a supreme donation of self from someone who did not have any doubts of his value.

SCHOOL

At about the age of four, children go to school, having mastered the abilities of separation from mother, a certain independence, command of language, the ability to take initiatives, play on their own, and up to a point become self-reliant. They are ready to acquire the three Rs. Now cognitive training begins in earnest.

Up to then their self-esteem, the feeling of being lovable, has grown through the parental nurturing, that is, on the child's ability to experience feelings of being recognised, wanted and appreciated. During the school years self-esteem will also be built on the results of industry and achievement. School, with its marks, reports and examination results, offers a visible indication of success or failure.

Self-esteem can now be built both from feeling loved by parents, and through the results of schoolwork, the beginning of industry. This dual basis of self-esteem, coming both from home and school, has important implications for adult love. If the child does not acquire the feeling of unconditional love on the basis of being a person in his or her own right, worthy of love, then love and approval become solely dependent on achievement. The consequence of this is that in adult relationships there is no expectation to be loved for one's own worth. Every bit of approval has to be earned through performance. The husband or the wife who have been brought up in this way expect only to be appreciated when they fulfil their roles at home and work. Their understanding of love is based on achievement, and they can enjoy approval only when they feel they have earned their approbation. Such men and women can become workaholics, keep extremely tidy and neat households. Their whole life of love is based on a routine contract. They expect to discharge their responsibilities to the full, and be praised or criticised according to results. They can be extremely critical of themselves and of their spouse if they fail to deliver the appropriate and required behaviour.

'IT IS NOT FAIR'

Between the ages of seven and ten children reach a point of development when they no longer accept the authority of their parents and teachers unconditionally. They begin to argue back, to question the parents' absolute authority, expect justifying reasons for rules and regulations, and feel treated unfairly when parents and teachers use their authority without adequate reason. These are the years when homes and classrooms reverberate with the sentence, 'It is not fair'.

The feeling of being asked to do something which does not respect one's integrity, or being treated exploitatively in any way, forms a deep groove in our emerging personality, and the whole sense of justice is linked with it. We expect to have our rights respected, to be treated fairly, our integrity safeguarded by everyone, but particularly by those who claim to love us. This is why we feel particularly hurt when we are

44

let down by those close to us, who, in failing us, elicit our deepest anger.

PUBERTY AND ADOLESCENCE

The beginning of the second decade is the time when puberty commences. The secondary sexual characteristics emerge, with the girl developing her breasts and vagina, with monthly menstruation, and the boy's voice breaks, hair appears on the face, and the genitalia develop. Nature has now prepared boys and girls to be physically attracted to each other, and to be mutually drawn for the sake ultimately of sexual intercourse.

It is the time when the separation between children and parents takes a further decisive step with the incest taboo. Puberty is the time of overt prohibition of incestuous relationships. Sadly these boundaries are sometimes broken by fathers and stepfathers, and sexual abuse occurs at puberty, or even before.

After the arrival of puberty, adolescence follows, lasting until the early twenties. It is a time when the final stage of autonomy takes place. Young people separate from their parents, find independent work or continue with higher studies, and begin to be interested sexually, usually in someone of the opposite sex.

This is the time when courtship starts, and we begin a series of emotional and sexual encounters until we find someone with whom we fall in love. Sometimes we fall in love with more than one person until one emerges as the chosen one, and marriage or cohabitation begins.

MARRIAGE

Men and women want to experience love from each other through marriage. Thus marriage becomes the second intimate relationship of love in life, and yet, instead of finding love, a number of marriages break up and end in divorce.

There are many reasons for divorce, but some of them are established in the course of our first intimate relationship of love when some people are hurt or wounded. These are emotional wounds which we carry into marriage, and there, in the intimacy of this second loving relationship, we relive the difficulties, frustrations and anger of our childhood experiences.

It is vital, therefore, to look at some of these common hurts and wounds in the next chapter.

6

Hurt Childhood

A normal childhood should give us the feeling that we are lovable and good, that is, we can emerge in adult life with a sufficient self-esteem to feel recognised, wanted and appreciated simply because we exist. Of course this experience does not excuse us from the task of working and further developing our potential, but everyone who has received unconditional love feels at least some of the above lovability. At the other end of the spectrum, we may feel unlovable, have low self-esteem and be very hungry for affection. In general there are small minorities at either end of the spectrum, with most people somewhere in the middle.

When we veer towards the negative side, we have difficulties in persuading ourselves that anyone wants or appreciates us. We are constantly surprised when people find us attractive and want our company. We feel shy and lack confidence, and are extremely grateful for the slightest notice given to us. We expect criticism, but when we receive it we are doubly hurt because we have no resources of good feelings to cushion it. We may get excessively angry at trivial upsets, shout and scream, or we may bury our anger and get depressed.

As hurt people, we are excited when we are befriended, but expect to be abandoned very easily. When we are receiving love, we feel that at long last our needs are being met, only to discover that we find it very difficult to register it, and push away those who love us or we test them continuously to ensure that they are genuine.

When these points are explained to men and women who have difficulties in their relationships, they are astonished. Some of them realise their childhood was not ideal, but they

47

still felt 'loved' by their parents. Others think it is their own fault, their parents gave them everything and it is they who made a mess of things.

In practice, of course, it is not always the parents' fault. In any case, fault is the wrong word. As parents they offered their children the best that was available at the time. But parents are not the only contributors to love. Genes play a part. Our capacity to receive love depends on our make-up, and some people can receive affirmation much more easily than others. So the love we feel as adults is a mixture of the parenting we receive and our genetic inheritance.

Nevertheless many are still surprised when they are faced with the possibility that their parents were not as loving as they thought they were. When they begin to examine the matter in detail they may find that, while their parents took care of them physically and educationally, in other words fed and clothed them, provided them with adequate material benefits and sent them to good schools, nevertheless they did not feel close to one or both parents.

The parents may have found it difficult to demonstrate affection and the children were rarely picked up, hugged or caressed. Feelings may rarely have been displayed. Both parents may have worked and had little time for them, or they were sent to boarding schools, against their wishes, from an early age. They may have had parents who never felt satisfied with their performance and, however successful they were, it was never good enough. Criticism may have been rampant, and appreciation or approval scarce. They may have felt ignored for long periods, and only noticed when they broke some rule.

Most people can recognise overt physical brutality, which nowadays is rare although it still exists. Many more wounds are inflicted by the absence of affection and affirmation in subtle ways, one of which, of course, is the fact that some parents prefer a brother or a sister to oneself.

Whatever the reason, there are a number of people who emerge from childhood without the experience of unconditional love, and this becomes a handicap when they are expecting to be loved, or when they try to love others.

48

More specifically, we can identify some particular patterns of hurt from individual phases of development.

DISORDERS OF ATTACHMENT

As we have already seen, the capacity to form a bond is fundamental to loving. There are people who find it difficult to form an attachment. For example, young people who suffer from autism, or adults with schizophrenic illnesses, are known to find it arduous to form relationships. Those who sufficiently overcome their problems and form an attachment live with the constant fear of losing their loved ones or being abandoned by them. They form what is known as 'anxious attachments'. The roots of jealousy and possessiveness are to be found in these anxious attachments. Such men and women live with the constant dread of being left, and every other person is a constant threat to their relationship. They imagine their spouse is having affairs when they are doing nothing of the sort, and they are overwhelmed with panic and desperation when they are. They expect to be supplanted with extraordinary ease, and all that the husband or wife has to do is to look at another woman or man, and there is hell to pay. Often such people are not only anxious about being abandoned, but they also live with the dread that something terrible will happen to their loved ones, so that if they are a little late in coming home they are overwhelmed with forebodings of tragedy.

Given this anxiety, they long to be physically close to their spouse, and when this is not possible, to be in telephone contact. Their hunger for physical closeness gives them the quality of being possessive for they dread to let their spouse out of their sight. Their partner feels a prisoner, and finds it very difficult to be or do things alone. The need for the physical presence of another person is a normal requirement of companionship, and is part of loving. The hunger for the presence of the spouse is the expression of excessive anxiety. Very often such an anxious person is satisfied with the mere physical availability of their spouse in the house. They rarely

49

want to do anything with them provided they are physically about. Thus they are often criticised by their partner who stays in the house, only to find their spouse asleep or busy with some activity, and not remotely interested in them.

The other attachment which has been described is the 'avoidant' one. Here the spouse finds it very difficult to tolerate closeness of any description. They want to be left alone and they remain aloof. They are busy with their own affairs, and they are often undemonstrative. They appear cold and disinterested, and like to keep their distance. Such an 'avoidant' person is in real difficulties especially when they are married to an anxious person who needs a great deal of closeness, but they remain problematic to normal personalities.

DISORDERS OF TRUST

Trust is fundamental for all human relationships, but particularly for those who are in an intimate loving exchange. In fact trust is essential for our survival. It is relevant to physical closeness. We need to feel that we are not going to be hurt by those to whom we entrust our body. Hence all physical and emotional violence is a violation of love. Since loving intimacy expects sexual intercourse, trust is essential at the moment we abandon all our defences and become united in coitus.

Emotionally trust is the foundation of the continuity of our loving relationship with another human being. If physical trust is the basis of our safety, then emotional trust is essential for the hope that we will continue to be loved.

Emotional trust may be strong or weak. If weak, such a person is suspicious, cynical, and expects very little out of life. They emerge from a childhood in which they had little reason to feel that anyone was reliable or trustworthy. Their parents promised but did not fulfil, were inconsistent, said one thing and did another, and told lies. They grew up expecting to be let down, and everybody is a potential source of further hurt.

This hurt is experienced particularly from those who are close to us when they fail to recognise, appreciate, or make us feel wanted. The possible range of feeling let down is infinite, but it shows particularly when the spouse has an affair. That is when trust vanishes. Regaining trust after an affair may be very difficult, and it may never return to the previous levels.

Trust is also essential in communication. If normal life is to continue, we must believe in those who relate to us, and particularly those who claim to love us. If they tell us lies, half truths, or hide essentials from us, the foundations are laid for distrust which is corrosive to a loving relationship. Very often we tell lies because we are afraid that we will hurt the person we love, or that they will be angry with us. When lie follows lie, the situation becomes unsustainable, and the final position is much worse than if we told the truth and faced the consequences.

DISORDERS OF AUTONOMY

Autonomy is linked with our freedom and independence. When we commit ourselves to love another person, our spouse, we are at the same time reducing our freedom to form an exclusive relationship with someone else and accepting the responsibility of faithfulness. Furthermore, central to loving is offering our availability. We offer our body, mind and feelings to the one to whom we make our exclusive commitment. These restrictions are self-imposed and are usually accepted as the necessary conditions for the unique loving intimacy of marriage.

But we may have problems in this area. We may have had parents who were domineering, possessive, exacting, demanding, overbearing, and our freedom and independence may have become extra-precious in our life. We may want the advantages of intimacy, but resent the restrictions on our freedom and independence, so, particularly in the early years of marriage, we enjoy sex, caring and affection, but want to go on as if we were single and use time to suit our purposes.

51

We go home for food and sex, and use the rest of the time to work, play and amuse ourselves with our friends. We have no time to meet the needs of our spouse. When she is critical, we become angry. When she requests something we interpret it as a demand. Such people treat their spouse as a restricting and demanding parent, against whom they angrily rebel.

Every satisfactory loving relationship has to work out a balance between availability and independence, dependence and autonomy, closeness and separation. On the one hand couples can be so close and dependent on each other that they are described as 'fused'. Such spouses cannot do anything independently, they rely entirely on each other and cling as well. Each loves 'by the kind permission of the other', feeling that they are incomplete without each other. On the other hand, they can be so independent that they hardly come near each other. Extremely independent relationships are the basis for the so-called 'open' marriages, in which the partners agree to have the freedom to have a series of extramarital relation-ships without the spouse minding. The trouble with such arrangements is that sooner or later one spouse begins to care and to feel jealous. Furthermore, while such arrangements are undertaken in the name of freedom, they are usually a mutual expression of the inability of accepting any limitation to freedom.

DISORDERS OF INDUSTRY

The point has been made already that self-esteem is built on the unconditional love given by the parents, and on the achievement of work which is preceded by school progress. When children lack the feeling of being loved on the basis of their intrinsic worth, they fall back on the conditional love which they earn through their industry. In adult life such relationships become contracts of mutual benefits. Instead of feeling wanted for their own sake, such spouses do things for each other on a contractual basis. They are saying to each other 'I will do this for you, if you do that for me.'

When for some reason such men or women are not in a

position to be productive, then they lose their self-esteem completely. If, for example, they are unemployed, they do not feel of any worth, and there is good evidence that marital breakdown is especially associated with unemployment. An alternative distortion is the person who works excessively as the whole basis for finding their value, and takes no pleasure in doing anything together with the partner or spending time with the children.

DISORDERS OF DEPENDENCE

The whole of childhood is a gradual separation from parental figures and those in authority. It is a covenant of gradual independence, in which the growing person learns to decide, cope, handle fear, plan, anticipate, and overcome threats to their survival. They emerge as autonomous, self-reliant, self-governing and self-directing.

Some people achieve physical and intellectual maturity without an equivalent emotional one. They look and behave as adults, but feel unsure, uncertain, frightened, and still feel they need to rely on somebody stronger than themselves.

Marriages between such an emotionally dependent person and someone who appears strong, dominant and assertive are common. The dependent person can be of either sex, and they marry for security in the widest sense of that word.

With the passage of time, such dependent people grow up and realise their emotional potential. They no longer need their partner to make decisions for them, where to go, what to do, to make up their minds, to shape their opinions and set their values. They no longer idealise or magnify the importance of their spouse. They can make an equivalent contribution to the relationship. This is the good outcome, but there are alternative and dangerous ones.

The commonest problem with such a relationship is that the dependent spouse will outgrow their parental partner. When they have attained their confidence, they will no longer need the security of their spouse. They do not need to live by kind permission of another. These are the men and women who claim they are no longer in love with their partner. Their 'love' was linked with their dependence. When that dependence disappears, so does their love, and the marriage comes to an end.

Another problem is that the so-called 'strong' person is in fact assertive, driving, domineering, but behind this 'strength' there may be an equally needy and emotionally deprived person. There comes the time when the dominant partner expresses their underlying needs and yearns for support, affection and understanding. These moments may come when they are sick, tired, under pressure or when things go wrong for them, when they lose a parent, friend or job. They make signals for help, but their partner neither recognises these, nor are they capable of giving succour. The dominant person is acceptable as long as they have no needs. If they do show their needy side, their dependent partner, who usually feels they have nothing to offer, is overwhelmed and may run away.

HEALTH

The majority of people are not seriously wounded. They proceed to their adolescence forming relationships, and sooner or later fall in love with a particular man or woman. In the next chapter I shall describe this state of falling in love.

7

Falling in Love

During adolescence a number of social and psychological situations occur which prepare young people to fall in love with one another. They have separated from their parents, that is, they experience aloneness. This aloneness sensitises them to the need of togetherness. Beyond togetherness, men and women long for an independent abode in which they can organise and control their lives. They want a home of their own. Cohabitation or marriage, particularly the latter, is a sign of adulthood. Through marriage they can assume adult roles. Society is organised around married adults, a state to which most people aspire.

Thus through aloneness, the desire of a home of one's own, and the authority and status that marriage confers, most people are propelled towards coupling.

There is the preliminary form of coupling in which a variety of men and women are sampled in the process of courtship. Young people form transitory relationships and find out whether they like the person they are with. They go to the pub, cinema, discos, concerts, outings, and they experiment with interacting. They assess whether they find each other sufficiently physically attractive, share the same ideas and outlook on life, want the same things and are comfortable with each other. There is excitement in finding out about these things.

Ultimately someone is preferred and becomes special. At this stage, two people fall in love with each other. Millions of words have been written to describe the state of being in love. It is a state of intense longing for union with another. Reciprocal love (union with the other) is associated with

55

fulfilment and ecstacy, unrequited love with emptiness, anxiety or despair. There are several essential aspects of falling in love.

At the heart of falling in love is physical attraction. Both sexes are highly attracted by each other's bodies. Although there is some agreement about physical beauty, there is no way that the special attraction of another's physical appearance can be defined. Attraction is based on a whole variety of factors, but it should be noted that vision, finding the other pleasing to the eyes, sound, being attracted by their voice, and touch, enjoying being held and stroked, are all essential. Physical excitation is thus stimulated by the same elements as those which form the attachment between ourselves and our mother. Falling in love is a resuscitation of the physical and emotional links which form our primary emotional attachment to mother, and it is a repeat in adult life of our infantile bonds.

But in addition to the gratification of vision, sound and touch, there is now an overall sexual dimension. Women and men now carry erotic excitation, and men long to touch the breasts and buttocks of women. Women are stimulated by general appearance of strength and the contours of the body. Both sexes, but particularly the man, are erotically aroused through touch, kissing and physical closeness, wanting ultimately sexual intercourse. The physical passion is intense.

Emotionally, couples need to be exclusively special to each other, to feel recognised, wanted and appreciated. The person they fall in love with makes them aware that they matter to each other, they are special. They feel needed and there is a mutuality of significance. When they meet each other everybody else fades into insignificance. Nobody else exists who is remotely comparable in importance, and the loved one occupies the centre of thoughts all the time. This occupation is intrusive, the person cannot be put out of one's mind.

Beyond physical and emotional attraction, there is social fitness. We are usually attracted by people who are of the same intelligence, interests and share our values and opinions. A number of problems arise when we find we are attracted physically to people who do not share the same interests or are not of the same background as ourselves. The conflict is between the heart and the head.

Thus we are usually attracted by someone we like physically, emotionally and socially. Once we have fallen in love we are in a state of emotional excitement, in some form of ecstacy, and several things happen in that state.

We tend to idealise the person we love. By idealisation is meant that we tend to think of our beloved as the most attractive, desirable and suitable person in the world. We are not in a mood to find fault with them. If we detect shortcomings, we reduce their importance. If the beloved upsets us, we tend to forgive and forget quickly. We want to believe that there is nothing wrong with the one we love.

The state of idealised excitement elicits a marked desire for closeness and contact. We spend hours on the telephone, write pages and pages of letters, and spend every possible moment with each other. There is an enormous longing for closeness, and especially for sexual intercourse.

This is the positive, ecstatic side of being in love. There is a negative, painful and depressive form. When the loved one is silent, withdrawn, or is reluctant to be as close as we want them to be, we fear that they are no longer interested in us and this causes deep distress. One moment is full of excitement and the next heralds despair.

When the telephone rings or the letter arrives, there is a great deal of excitement. The passionate response can actually involve the body with the heart beating fast, the muscles getting tense, flushing of the face, and even sweating. There is a state of profound physiological arousal. The body trembles with excitement at the anticipation of even momentary closeness. Thoughts cannot be controlled, they are obsessed with the beloved. There is a strong feeling that they prefer to be with their special boy or girl rather than anybody else. Concentration on work becomes difficult because the person is preoccupied with the beloved.

In the presence of such intensity of love, the fear of losing the loved one is a very real one. Hence there are moments of intense jealousy when he or she looks at someone else or even temporarily abandons the relationship for another person.

The scorn that is poured on the intruder is immense because it is difficult to conceptualise anyone more attractive than oneself.

To sum up, love and romance seem to be one of, if not the most, powerful activator of our pleasure centres. Both tend to be very exciting emotionally. Being with the person, or even just thinking of them, is highly stimulating. Being in love is, by definition, the strongest positive feeling we can have. Other things, stimulant drugs, passionate causes, manic states, can induce powerful changes in our brains, but none so reliably, so enduringly, or so delightfully, as that 'right' other person. If the relationship is not established securely, or is uncertain, anxiety or other displeasure centres may be quite active as well, producing a situation of great emotional turmoil as the lover swings between hope and torment.

Being in love is not a state that can last for ever. Couples decide to bring the agony of separation to a close and live together in the form of cohabitation, or usually marriage. While the ardour of feelings may last for years for some couples, the intensity usually wanes and the couple enter a period of 'loving' which may last up to fifty years or more.

When it comes to loving, we know very little of its components. What is it that keeps a couple together for such a long time? In the next three chapters I describe what I consider three essential components of loving based on observation and clinical experience.

8

Loving – I
Sustaining

There is widespread evidence that the ecstacy which is experienced during the stage of falling in love is shortlived. The high state of emotion subsides and the couple have to survive on a different basis of mutuality. I have chosen four characteristics which I consider essential for the sustaining aspect of loving. These are availability, communication, demonstration of affection and resolution of conflict.

AVAILABILITY

Mention has been made several times of the fact that human beings, like the higher animals, form attachments to each other. These are based on vision, seeing each other, sound, hearing one another and touching each other's bodies. During the stage of being in love, there was an intensification of this togetherness. Togetherness remains a key factor in availability. The fact of seeing, hearing and touching gives one intense gratification, and so being in the presence of each other remains a regular need for couples.

There are a number of difficulties which operate against this togetherness. Men and women are busy during the day with their work, and when they come home in the evening they are occupied with the children, cooking the evening meal and clearing up. By that time it is late, and they want to go to bed. Thus they are not available to each other. In bed one or both may read, and in this way they do not interact with each other.

But there are other reasons for not spending time together. The working schedule may be such that the couple leave early in the morning and arrive home late at night. If they manage to come home early, very often they spend the evening entertaining, going out with friends, or being in the pub. At the weekends there are things to catch up on, shopping to do, jobs about the house, or office work continued on Saturday and Sunday. Couples who entertain, or are entertained a lot, never have private access to one another.

It is imperative that some time be allocated when the couple are with their children and alone with each other. This is the time to be still and be aware of the partner, to simply gaze and take notice of a new dress, hair style, suit, and admire it. So often spouses ignore these small but important changes in the other's style of life. A moment's recognition gives the feeling that one exists. Women in particular, but both sexes, have to guard against being taken for granted. The wife soon feels that she is a mere housekeeper, and the husband only a provider. Nowadays women tend to work and feel that they put their incomes into the home and remain housekeepers as well. The moment of personal awareness is important to shake the nightmare of non-being. Couples can be so busy struggling for survival that they have no time for each other.

Another form of availability is the togetherness of accomplishing a shared task. Clearing the table and washing up together are probably the commonest shared tasks. Decorating the house or gardening can be carried out together. Shopping can be a weekly event for the couple. In all these activities there is the pleasure of being in each other's presence and accomplishing a task. This togetherness also reassures that the couple are going to stay together and are planning for a future together.

This togetherness must also take into consideration what has been said already, that couples need a balance of togetherness and separateness. This separateness is usually achieved by being at work when the couple are apart. But there are moments at the weekend when one or the other wants to be alone for a while. This has to be respected. The modern term is giving space to each other. This space can be occupied by playing a sport, gardening, constructing things, reading or listening to music. The right balance between closeness and separateness has to be worked out for each couple, and may alter at stages of their life. What is important, however, is that, while the rhythm of this tension is preserved, nevertheless the couple are available to one another when they are needed.

Which takes us to the next experience of availability, namely developing the presence of the appropriate empathy. By empathy I mean an awareness of the inner world of the other person, and the ability to respond accurately to the need of the moment. The awareness of the inner world of the spouse is a matter of reading accurately their mood. If the mood is one of distress, then it is important to enquire what is the nature of the distress. Is it the sadness of losing a friend, or hearing the news of illness of someone who matters or the disappointment of something not achieved, or frustration at something having gone wrong? The commonest feeling that we have to respond to is the apprehension, anxiety and fear of our partner. It is an acutely painful sensation, and availability means that we relieve the discomfort.

The ability to discern the inner world of our partner depends on our ability to know our spouse well, anticipate their reaction and read the cues they give us accurately. They may look sad, apprehensive, full of joy, or be shaking with fear. To be read accurately by those who love us is a reminder of the earliest experiences of our life when mother or father knew our inner world instinctively, even before language arrived. Later on we love to be surprised by being given a sympathetic and appreciative comment by our partner to a real need inside us without having to spell it out. It gives us the feeling of real closeness and being properly understood. It shows us that our partner is in touch with us and wants to reach us before we call out.

This high degree of empathy is not widely available. Most of the time we need to be informed what is going on, but we relish the moments when we are reached spontaneously.

Beyond the availability of togetherness, task-orientation,

61

and empathy, there is the presence of the spouse at key moments of our life. When couples recount the accumulation of distressing experiences which have brought them to the point of wanting to separate, the absence or neglect of their partner at a key moment of their life plays an important role.

Times of illness or experiences of pain are one of these key moments. It should be remembered that when we are very young and acutely dependent on our attachment figure for survival, physical or emotional distress are crucial experiences that made us run back to our key figure. Throughout childhood and adult life, we are encouraged to cope with illness and distress by being brave and keeping a stiff upper lip. Psychology has taught us that it is better to show our emotions and seek comfort when we need it without, of course, turning into hypochondriacs. Illness is a time when we not only experience discomfort but, if serious, our very survival is at stake. At these times we regress to an earlier stage of our life, and we need to be picked up and comforted. Most spouses are in fact likely to respond with sensitivity and care to illness, and look after each other when they are incapacitated, but there are a few who run away from illness. They find it frightening and feel helpless before it. Instead of being supportive and nurturing, they turn their backs and disappear. Very often the person who cannot cope is the husband, but sometimes women can react in this way. Another negative response is to attack the sick person and blame them for their illness on the ground that they did not take enough care of themselves. Sometimes the sick person does not want to be fussed over, and they repulse all attention, but normally we become dependent when we are sick and we look for a facilitating response from our partner.

Illness is closely allied to death. Spouses lose their parents at any time, but they themselves are usually in their forties and fifties when this happens. The illness and death of a parent is another key moment of availability. The sickness that has preceded for months or years is a time when the spouse is stretched in their resources. They need the support of their partner. This support may mean transport, looking after the children while the spouse is away, having the elderly

62

parent at home, visiting in the hospital, or actually nursing them. All this imposes a great deal of strain on the couple. It is a moment of heightened need, and most partners respond generously, but not all. There is the spouse who complains of the absences of their partner, busy visiting or nursing the elderly parent. They do not want to be left alone or to take care of themselves. They urge their spouse to put their parent into care, and under no circumstances are they prepared to have them in their home. These acts of obstruction are very painful, and are interpreted as callousness.

At the time of death the bereaved spouse needs time to grieve. That is to say, they need time to cry as a protest against the loss, a reminder of the way the young child protests at its mother's absence. This is followed by searching as the baby did for mother, the actual visiting of the grave if buried, and finally, the long period of detachment when they get accustomed to the loss by internalising the deceased person.

At the other end of the scale, there are the moments of creativity and joy. This begins with the delivery of the newborn. While labour has its painful moments, in general giving birth is an exciting and happy experience. The mother wants to share it with her husband. Nowadays this is possible in the majority of circumstances. There is no excuse for the husband to be missing. Most husbands do not, of course, miss the occasion, but some do. They are not in the country, are travelling, or, much worse, they are found drunk in the pub celebrating in anticipation with their mates. The absence of the father from the birth of the child is an event which is remembered for the whole lifetime, and brought up later on when some further adverse complications occur in the relationship.

Another joyous event (for some!) is the birthday. It is a special moment, and it means a lot when it is remembered. It shows that a special time in the life of the spouse is recollected and commemorated by a suitable gift. The day calls for a celebration. Wives rarely forget birthdays or wedding anniversaries, but husbands sometimes do, and this anniversary can be painful. It is not that the day is forgotten as such, but that the person has been ignored. Finally, holidays are a special time. They are a period of renewal for the couple who combine all the factors of availability, the togetherness, doing things, a high degree of empathy of what pleases each other, and time to realise it. Sadly holidays can be spoiled by arguing about the activities, being mean about the expenses and difficult about doing the things that please one another.

Availability is the key to loving in that its various forms remind the couple of the ever-present presence of mother or father in childhood, coupled with the safety and security that togetherness presented. It is the principal feature of exclusivity, and it brings about the daily unity of the couple. When it is freely present, spouses can bask in the knowledge that they exist for each other, and the strength that this gives makes them available to their children and to others. When it is present, it is taken for granted, but it causes acute distress when it is missing.

COMMUNICATION

The next stage beyond availability is verbal communication. There are major differences between men and women when it comes to communication. Women are simply very much better at it. In fact, when men cannot cope with women's talk they call it nagging! There are other differences as well. Men stress the reason component, whereas women are more concerned with feelings and intuition. These contrasting approaches lead to extended arguments in homes all over the world as the men argue their case as they understand it logically, and women respond with their feelings and intuition. At its best this encounter between the sexes is creative and produces a rich result. This observation does not mean for one moment that women are not capable of reason, or men of feelings and intuition. There are many exceptions to the rule. At its worst, when the complementarity is not appreciated, all the couples do is to argue and disagree, calling each other wrong. They are not wrong; they are simply expressing different facets of the truth.

Another aspect of communication is the ability of the listener to make sense of what the other is saying when the verbalising spouse is confused. The partner who is listening can discern patterns of meaning which the speaker cannot.

This discerning depends on the ability to listen carefully to the partner. Sometimes we are so keen to have our say that we are not paying attention to what our spouse is saying. We simply want them to stop talking so that we can start. When we do listen, do we do so non-judgmentally? That is, do we keep quiet until we hear something we do not approve of, then make a judgmental remark? Do we in fact pepper our response with criticism of our spouse, or do we affirm them? We are very good at affirming children, but we forget that adults need praise as well. It is only too easy to forget to give thanks for or appreciate meals, the routine that keeps the house clean, the care of children, the sweat of work, all in fact daily routine procedures.

Communication needs to be clear, shared, non-judgmental, appreciative and informative. It is another essential part of loving, and there is a grave handicap when it is not available, as in the case of the person who has had a stroke and loses the use of their speech.

But, of course, communication can have its negative side, when we shower abuse on each other. By the time that point is reached, the relationship is in bad shape and needs counselling.

DEMONSTRATION OF AFFECTION

Couples need to experience recurrent demonstration of affection from each other, apart from having sexual intercourse. I have often seen couples who come to counselling in which the wife says 'He never tells me he loves me' and he replies 'I told you I loved you twenty-five years ago. Why do you want to hear it again? I am still here, aren't I?' This exchange is another reminder that there are differences in the sexes in this area as well. Women are far more keen to demonstrate and receive affection. Feelings are not confined to

65

communication. The kiss, a hug, a touch are peak instants, in which the couple are sharing a moment of intimacy. Spouses want to be told that they love one another. The demonstration of affection is distinctive of the couple who are in touch with the inner world of each other. In this way they are showing to each other that they remain special.

Men sometimes become embarrassed by demonstrations of affection, feeling that it is unmanly, while women cherish the moment they are touched as a signal of special awareness. One of the constant complaints of women is that their men will not make a special fuss of them unless they want to have sex. In fact some wives know that sex is wanted because they get special attention on that day.

But if men are not always good at direct demonstration of affection, they may show it indirectly by buying things for their wives or doing suitable actions. The trouble is that wives, while they may get excited with jewellery, chocolates and flowers, do not want to be bought. In addition to the provision of things, they want to be cherished with words and/or action.

Being held in the arms of one's spouse is a reminder of the way we were held in the arms of our mother. In our childhood we experienced cherishing in the arms of our parents, an appreciation that was reinforced by being kissed. Puberty has eroticised the same behaviour, but affection remains the infrastructure of its meaning, and recurrent expression is a constant need for couples, as it is for children. Such warm, affectionate exchange can often become the prelude to sexual intercourse, but it has a validity of its own.

RESOLUTION OF CONFLICT

No one needs reminding that the opposite side of the coin of love and intimacy is conflict. When a couple live in the modern atmosphere of egalitarian relationships there is bound to be conflict when they disagree, hurt, and are aggressive towards each other. Under these circumstances there is often a victor and vanquished. Either partner can win the argument and feel vindicated, but, at the heart of a loving relationship, conflict is not about victory or defeat; it is about getting closer to each other. When we feel angry it is because we have not been heard, we have been misunderstood, we feel rejected, ignored or let down. We shout and scream or show our upset quietly. The whole point of such an expression of anger is not to win a point, but to have a point of view registered. Our anger is mobilised because we have been hurt, and a constructive quarrel is one in which the partner registers the pain we have experienced. The anger should be a signal for us to avoid the distress we have caused. Ideally, as our moments of anger are understood, the occasions for outbursts should decrease in frequency. In fact, when we find our quarrelling is escalating, then there is a fundamental problem in the relationship and help should be sought.

A constructive quarrel is also one which is not only followed by forgiveness and resolution of tension, but we should also aim to discover the vulnerability of our partner and try to help them overcome their difficulty. In the above instance, quarrelling should lead us to try to avoid repeating the pattern of inciting controversy. In the latter case our aim should be to help our partner overcome their difficulty.

This leads us to the second aspect of loving, which is our attempt to heal our spouse, that is, to provide them with the means of overcoming their difficulties, which is the subject of the next chapter.

9

Loving – II
Healing

The main thrust of this book is that there are historic forces operating in western society imposing a high degree of intimacy in the lives of couples. There is in addition a high percentage of wounded people who emerge from their childhood with difficulties in experiencing intimacy. These have been referred to in Chapter 6. To a greater or lesser extent we are all wounded people, but some are more so than others.

In the last hundred years psychoanalysis has taught us that there are ways of responding to hurt people which give them a chance of healing. These are second chances which a few people obtain through psychoanalysis and psychotherapy. At the heart of psychoanalysis are two models of change. The first and classical one is transference. In this reaction the patient experiences the analyst as a parental figure and relives through him earlier childhood experiences which are interpreted by the therapist and thus the patient can learn new ways of feeling which are more appropriate for the effective functioning of the adult self. The second model is dependent partially on this exchange, but even more on learning from the personality of the therapist a more effective way of being.

Very few people can undergo analysis or therapy, but the majority of human beings enter the depths of intimacy of marriage. There they can experience their spouse as a parental figure and, provided the right interaction takes place, there is a second chance of learning at this level of the relationship. This is one basis of healing. There are others.

There are two other forms of healing current in psychology. The first is behaviour therapy. There are many aspects to this therapy, but basically behaviour is shaped by rewards and punishments. This is in fact how most of us relate to each other. When we are pleased with what we experience we reward the person, and in this way encourage the repetition of the particular conduct. The reward can take any form in marriage, from praise to sexual intercourse, whatever pleases the partner. When the behaviour is unpleasant or painful, then we respond in a punitive manner. In marriage, spouses withdraw from each other, and either withhold behaviour that pleases or actually deliver something unpleasant. In ordinary life the behaviouristic model is the one which operates most commonly. We are pleased when things go well, and angry when they do not.

There is a third model based on cognitive therapy. In this approach we appeal to the learning mechanism of another person to see that what they are experiencing, saying or doing is wrong, and we offer alternative ways of seeing things. This is an attempt to change people by appealing to their understanding of life.

Spouses can work in all three ways with their partners. First of all they can try and understand how they are experienced as parental figures. Women find it far more easy to see themselves in the role of mother, and to see their husband as a little boy, despite their manly appearance and conduct. Husbands find it more difficult to see themselves as fathers, with their wives in the role of little girls. But there is no doubt that both partners can continue in the parental role. It is important to assess the parental role that one has been put in, and to avoid colluding with the expectations. In other words one should aim at making the partner responsible for his or her own life and not avoid the task of growing up by making decisions for them, making up their minds or stepping in and doing the things they find difficult.

The second thing each partner should recognise is the defences that their spouse has developed. Dynamic psychology has shown that each one of us creates a distinctive way of protecting ourselves psychologically from anxiety and pain. Initially Freud concentrated on the defences to which we resort to guard ourselves from unacceptable aggression and sexuality; but we build up defences to cover up a wide range of painful experiences. We use the mechanisms of denial, projection, rationalisation, among others which are unconscious, to avoid facing painful realities. We deny responsibility for our actions, fears, aggressive feelings, or that we are lustful. We say that it is not us, but our partner who is entertaining these ideas, or we offer some trite explanation for our conduct.

It is vital in healing to recognise what defence our spouse is using. This is not difficult because it is repetitive and predictable. When they feel angry they deny it. When they feel guilty but will not own up, they will project their guilt on their partner. When they are caught in some malpractice, they will offer some trivial explanation.

Handling the repetitive defences of our spouse is a special task of healing. The mistake we make is to resort to moralistic language. When our partner repeatedly denies some damaging action they perform, we call this failure to own up lying. When they offer an explanation of why they cannot do something we have asked them to do, we call them lazy. When they put their interest before ours, we call them selfish, instead of finding out why they find it difficult to be generous.

The homes of millions of couples reverberate with this moralistic language, which is tossed to and fro as a form of abuse: 'Oh, my husband is lazy, selfish, self-centred, and a liar too'. These accusations are constantly present in counselling sessions. What is needed is to exercise the patience to discover why the spouse is behaving in this particular way, using a particular defence, and gently confront him or her with reality. If spouses are accused in moral terms, they simply dig their heels in, further protecting their character. The debate shifts from finding what is really wrong to mutually protecting their self esteem from each other's attacks.

An essential part of healing is to avoid using moralistic language, and persisting in confronting their partner with their defences. When this has been achieved, then help is given to overcome the particular difficulty. These difficulties are associated with anxiety, fear, lack of initiative, self-esteem, in general the fear that they cannot cope with something in

70

life which is avoided or the easier route is taken. The husband says he has had no time to carry out the request of his wife when he has forgotten due to a persistent poor memory, to which he cannot own up. When he asks his wife to telephone the garage or builder and have an argument over the bill, it is because he cannot face arguments. Another perennial difficulty is that of asking things for oneself because we find it difficult to believe that others will want to please us. Another difficulty many have is of saying no to requests they get in case they upset the person who has asked the favour. All of us have a whole lot of small or big difficulties, for which we make excuses. The trouble is we are compliant with strangers with whom, for example, we never lose our temper, only to come home and let loose an almighty rage. This is the defence of displacement. We usually displace our anger from those we fear to those with whom we are familiar. Thus wives can complain of husbands who will do anything for the neighbour, but never put up a shelf in her own home, or start the conversion of the kitchen, which remains unfinished while the rest of the street has been redecorated, all this coming from the person who cannot say no. While the wife is sweet to all her friends, she is a mass of frustration and anger at home where everything irritates her. A fine example of displacement.

Couples are indeed loving each other when they recognise the parental role they are being put in and refuse to accept it, or do so for a while with their eyes open to what they are doing, following which they recognise the specific defence their spouse uses, understand what anxiety, fear, anger it is hiding, and confront that reality instead of bombarding their partner with moralistic language which is a form of destructive abuse leading to a cul-de-sac in the relationship.

If couples can do these two things consistently from the beginning of their relationship, the way to healing has begun.

When the confrontation with the fear, anxiety or anger is made the next step is not to humiliate the spouse for having such a trait. It is not considered a weakness, nor is a judgmental approach made. The anxiety is recognised and the spouse is encouraged to face and overcome it. This will not take

71

place at once. The diffident person will not suddenly summon the courage to be angry or say no to requests, but a start can be made, and every time a success is scored it is rewarded so that the new learning takes root in the personality.

In this way some of the commonest anxieties, such as lack of confidence and low self-esteem, can be overcome when the spouse is systematically encouraged to give up avoidance techniques, such as not taking on the challenges or stopping apologising continuously for one's existence. At the heart of these two problems is the feeling that one is not lovable or worthwhile. Everybody is worthwhile, and the spouse can give his wife or her husband the feeling of unconditional acceptance, and slowly encourage them to believe in themselves. Healing in these instances is a matter of giving nurturing and succour to somebody who needs it, and at the same time encouraging them to undertake new challenges with the confidence that they will succeed.

If the spouse comes from a deprived background, then they are hungry for affection, and if this is the problem their spouse can be generous in their sustaining of them.

This healing is relatively easy when one spouse is wounded and the other is more stable and mature and has a loving disposition. It becomes more difficult when both parties are wounded people. Even so, their wounds are not likely to be similar, and they can give each other support where they need it most.

After this general introduction of moving from moralising and guilt-producing onslaught to an understanding of the anxiety that determines behaviour, coupled with intensified sustaining for lack of self-esteem and deprivation, we can move to some specific problems.

DISORDERS OF ATTACHMENT

I have mentioned that about 25 per cent of people form anxious attachments, and about the same number the avoidant form. Let us look at both these problems.

People with anxious attachments are constantly afraid of

losing the person they are close to. Such a person tends to cling to their mate, be jealous and possessive and fearful that they will lose their partner to someone else. Short of losing them, they are apprehensive about them being injured or falling ill.

The response to the person with the anxious attachment is initially to ensure that they are not made unduly anxious. If they are terrified of losing their partner to another man or woman, there is no point in their spouse flirting or becoming excessively involved with another person. Their partner should try to be as reliable and punctual as possible, and make the spouse feel secure.

But there are limits which should be set to this anxious behaviour. If the anxious partner is restrictive and possessive, that is, attempts to stop the partner from going out, having friends or activities outside the home, this should not be tolerated. Every care should be taken to encourage the anxious person to overcome their fear by spending periods away from home, allowing their partner to do likewise and undertaking sole activities.

A basic anxiety of such a person is the fear of disintegration that will ensue if they are left alone. In order to overcome this fear they should be encouraged to be less dependent on their partners and learn to cope and fend for themselves. The person with anxious attachment has to gain inwardly a sense of greater confidence in their capacity to survive by themselves in case they lose their partner, and that means stretching their potential while their spouse is alive and available. Their spouse can avoid ridiculing their fear of loss and encouraging self-reliance in every possible way.

The avoidant attachment is the person whose anxiety is not about loss but about closeness. They are afraid of intimacy which feels like an intrusion. They keep their distance, avoid emotional contact, are reserved and do not let people get close to them. Closeness is very threatening and they remain aloof.

Such a person is not easy to know. they are genuinely afraid of closeness and they do not want to be touched or to become emotionally involved. They can be criticised for being 'stuck up'. In fact, behind this veil of aloofness, they yearn for companionship.

The response to such a person is to try to reach them as far as they will allow it. After that, every effort should be made to overcome their resistance by making emotional contact rewarding. Their partner can encourage short periods of physical closeness, touch, kissing, hugging, first in private and then gradually in public. The whole point about the avoidant attachment is that he or she has to learn how to experience physical intimacy safely.

Spouses married to an avoidant personality complain that they are cold and distant and that the only time they get close is when they want sex. One way of helping them overcome their difficulty is by encouraging them to be physically close before sex so that they can conquer their hesitation for intimacy.

DISORDERS OF TRUST

Some men and women grow up with a very low level of trust. Such people are suspicious, mistrustful, afraid that they will be let down and at times become paranoid, that is, they expect others to have malevolent intentions towards them. When these suspicions become set beliefs, not open to reason, they become delusions which are held tenaciously.

When anxious attachment is coupled with mistrust, a psychiatric syndrome of morbid jealousy develops in which the spouse is absolutely convinced that their partner is having an affair with someone, even if there is no shred of evidence supporting such a view. Morbid jealousy is rare, but it plays havoc with a marriage relationship as the partner is certain that their spouse is having an affair, and shouts and screams about it. They are so convinced of their suspicions that they engage private agents to follow their spouse, they examine their clothes for evidence of perfume, hairs or lipstick, and they trace their moves with incredible detail, convinced that they are having secret assignations. Morbid jealousy is not open to reason as it is a delusion, but the spouse who is accused can do everything possible to reassure their spouse, spend as much time with them as possible and, of course, avoid any incriminating behaviour. The important thing is that the partner who is accused needs to understand the nature of the problem, otherwise they become convinced that they are going crazy.

The mistrustful person does not extend their suspicions to such a degree, but they tend to be secretive and guarded. They will keep their papers locked up, they will hide the things that matter to them from their partners. They are reluctant to disclose their inner world in case the information they reveal is used against them. These are people who are described as keeping their cards close to their chest.

The mistrustful person is not easy to reach. They need to be reassured that their confidence will not be betrayed. At the same time they have to be confronted about their anxieties. Basically they are afraid that if they reveal their inner world its contents will not be respected, and worse, it will be exploited. These fears have to be challenged. They need to be trained to discern between people they can trust, such as their spouse, and others who may let them down. In building up trust the spouse has to be careful not to promise beyond their capacity so they do not let their partner down and reinforce their fears.

Building up trust is a slow process, but it enlarges the horizons of both spouses as they reveal more and more of themselves to each other, with the certainty that their confidences will be respected.

DISORDERS OF AUTONOMY

At the heart of disorders of autonomy is to be found the man or woman who grew up in a home dominated by one or both parents. For years they had to submit their will to parental wishes out of fear, or the threat of being dismissed or humiliated. They grew up resenting such authority, and they refuse to take orders from anybody. The trouble with such a spouse is that the simplest request is interpreted as a demand. They cannot distinguish the natural requirements expected of them to fulfil their roles from unreasonable and authoritarian commands.

Clearly such a person is extremely sensitive to any approach made to them. The tone of the request is vital, and their co-operation should first be sought before anything is asked of them. A request can be preceded by the clear indication that it is not a demand.

But life has to go on, and the spouse has to have a clear discussion with their partner that they are not behaving as authoritarian figures but simply asking what is necessary for survival. An understanding should be reached which distinguishes the spouse from the parent figure, and encourages requests to be treated on their own merits. This is achieved more quickly if the spouse handles the sensitive partner with respect, listens to their opinion, and pays attention to it, and generally considers them as responsible adults which dilutes the feeling of being treated as an incompetent child. Of course care should be taken in such common situations as driving a car, not to be a back seat driver, not to take pleasure when a mistake has been made, and to avoid appearing to correct the partner every other second.

DISORDERS OF DEPENDENCE

The whole aim of development is to finish up as an adult who is reasonably autonomous, self-reliant and self-directing. There are many people who attain intellectual and physical adulthood, but remain dependent and passive emotionally. Such a man or woman often marries an apparently domineering, assertive, competent partner, and there is a collusion between the two, already mentioned, which can prove disastrous for the relationship when the dependent person matures and no longer needs their strong partner. The secret of a successful outcome is for the so-called 'strong' partner to realise what is going on early in the relationship and to encourage their partner to grow up.

That means in practice that, when appealed to for advice,

the pros and cons of a situation are discussed but the decision is taken by the dependent partner. Even more subtly, when a request for advice or an opinion is made, the request is turned around with the question 'What do you think?'

Every attempt is made to engage in dialogue, but leaving decisions to the dependent person. In the same way, when they ask that things be done for them which they are afraid to do, an attempt should be made to encourage them to tackle the object of their fear rather than taking over parts of their life.

Every step of independence in learning to drive a car, take initiatives, learn to handle the finances, make decisions about everyday matters, or holidays, should be encouraged.

In general the dependent person should be supported and encouraged to tackle the things they are afraid to do, and be rewarded as they achieve a new step of independence.

This is the opposite approach from the one in which the strong partner controls and regulates the life of their dependent spouse. In fact the strong partner should not be afraid to show from the very beginning that they too have needs which their partner should make every effort to meet.

DISORDERS OF MATURITY

The dependent person is a frightened child. The immature spouse is an irresponsible child clothed in adult garments. These people crowd psychiatric clinics, the law courts, the world of gambling and alcoholism. They have most commonly been called psychopaths. Their characteristics are the need for immediate gratification because they cannot tolerate frustration. They are very sensitive to criticism, with excessive and unreasonable outbursts of anger. They often resort to physical violence and are prone to sulk. They tend to lie because they are terrified of responsibility of any sort. It is out of the ranks of such personalities that gamblers, alcoholics and the sexually irresponsible emerge. They also have unstable work records, always promising and expecting some grand achievement, but on the whole being very poor performers

77

with little capacity to stick to anything and overcome difficulties. They can often be charming, promising the moon and delivering very little. They can be belligerent one moment and crying on their knees, begging for another chance the next. Clearly not all those characteristics are to be found in the same person, but most of them show a cluster which has the unmistakable stamp of this particular type of personality.

Immature people clutter the Divorce Courts under the category of unreasonable behaviour, and the Church tribunals for nullity.

In the presence of such a person it may be thought that the best thing to do is give up and try afresh. Many spouses resort to this reaction, and no one can blame them.

If an attempt is made to try to cope with such immaturity then the only tenable response is kindness, coupled with firmness. It has to be realised that one is dealing with an irresponsible child, only they are adults. Firmness is the only way out. Such men and women have to be reprimanded for their bad conduct, told in no uncertain terms that aggression will not be tolerated, and that they will only be rewarded if they behave themselves. A certain number of such people do mature with the passage of time, but they do present hard work.

In the following categories of disorders we are in the world of frank psychiatry. This is not a textbook of treatment of psychological disorder, but two conditions, anxiety and depression, are so common that something has to be said about them.

ANXIETY

Mention has already been made of anxious attachment. When the anxiety is more generalised, and this is an extremely common trait, the person is apprehensive about losing their partner, their future, their prospects, and especially their health. They live their lives with constant anxiety about their survival, even though they can be, and usually are, loving, responsible, and in every other respect normal people.

When the anxiety reaches a very high level, it is accompanied by irritability, mood swings, a number of physical symptoms, and a high level of apprehension. Anxiety is a very common phenomenon, and the waiting rooms of doctors are full of anxious men and women who find it difficult to cope with life.

Loving an anxious partner is a matter of being infinitely patient with their worries. One moment it is time for reassurance, and the next for being jocular and getting them out of their predicament by a lighthearted approach. Anxiety cannot be ignored, but at the same time such people should be encouraged to live full lives and helped to overcome their common fears of travelling, being away from home or tackling new situations. They should be listened to but encouraged to switch off and leave their preoccupations well alone. They are often afraid of dying and, while no one can guarantee certainty of life from moment to moment, they can be almost invariably reassured that their moment of departure has not arrived. If the symptoms become excessive, and take the form of severe phobias or obsessional manifestations which are crippling, then, of course, expert help must be sought.

Many spouses live happily with their anxious partners by treating their fears always with care and attention, and responding to them with a mixture of gentle cajoling and humour. Nowadays a whole array of relaxation techniques exist, including Yoga and meditation, to which anxious people can resort with great advantage.

DEPRESSION

After anxiety, the commonest psychological difficulty is a depressive mood. Depression has been known since ancient times, and is a disorder which affects the mind, giving the person a sense of misery, gloom, lack of energy and enthusiasm, irritability, and the desire to withdraw from life and other people, including the spouse. Most depressive illnesses are nowadays recognised and treated successfully, usually

79

with medication, but some are chronic in nature and very persistent.

Living with a person who is subject to depression can be a trying experience because of their withdrawal and apathy. They do not want to talk, go out, socialise, or be in any way available. Their partner is isolated and feels as if they are completely alone.

It is essential that the true nature of the depression is understood, otherwise the sufferer is thought to be lazy, inconsiderate, uncivil and uncaring. It is no good pretending that they can be mobilised by being made to feel guilty, or shaken out of their lethargy. The condition is very real and debilitating.

What is needed is a combination of genuine sympathy and gentle encouragement to undertake activity and participate in events. While the withdrawal should be respected, the temperature of the water should be regularly tested and any indication of the lightening of mood encouraged. The spouse has to live within the reality of depression and the unceasing vigilance to encourage life and activity.

As with the case of anxiety, severe depression, and any threat of suicide, should be taken seriously and radical help sought.

Loving entails responding accurately and sensitively to the personality of our spouse. Psychology has focused more clearly on various aspects of the personality, although its principal features have always been recognised. In the past, however, the adverse features were joined to a moral approach and the person was invited to change out of fear of punishment, or the sense of guilt. Both these feelings are no longer considered desirable as instruments of transformation. Instead spouses expect to be understood, reached and loved and, whenever possible, to be given second chances to restore their integrity. This is a rich field of Christian action, for at the centre of our faith lies loving which restores wholeness. In practice there is no institution which offers so much chance for healing as the intimate relationship of marriage. So, armed with our modern psychological insight, we face a new era of healing over the fifty years of married life.

This healing requires the undertaking of continuity, stability and reliability, for without these the conditions do not exist for healing. Time is needed to appraise the situation, and patience is required for the appropriate response to work. Christianity has to offer the world this healing pattern against the conclusion of relationships when difficulties appear and the insistence of starting afresh with someone else. The new spouse will only produce a different set of problems. The point is stressed again and again that modern intimacy is a conflict-generating condition, and all marriages have to be continuously worked at.

This work extends to the third factor, which involves change over time, and the next chapter will deal with this.

10

Loving – III
Growth

Nowadays couples can be expected to live together for some fifty years or more. There are those who claim that no two people can endure each other for such a period and that change is necessary. Boredom is offered as one of the reasons for divorce. In fact if a couple are offering to each other the right ingredients in their social, emotional, sexual, intellectual and spiritual life, they do not want to change. A marital relationship is a major investment of one's life, and it should not be lightly discarded if the spouse is mutually compatible. A new partner might be more exciting, but every relationship needs a good deal of energy expounded to make it work, and so the original effort should be carefully nurtured. In addition it is exciting to see the person with whom one lives change and grow. Loving implies that one can live with the change and assist the partner to realise their potential, in other words be a facilitator. Of course one of the factors that keeps the majority of couples together is their children, but children come and go, and the constant factor is each other.

When it comes to describing change and growth, the one thing we are certain of is that they happen; but our understanding of the detailed mechanism of how these two factors occur is far from complete.

At the heart of change is the life-cycle of married life. This can be described in terms of the period before the first child arrives. Life changes with the arrival of the first, second and third child; then entry into primary school, then secondary school, their adolescence, the departure of the first child, until the last child leaves, and then the couple return to their original dyad state. Each of these phases demands specific requirements from parents, and challenges them to respond to their growing children.

There are other social and biological changes, such as entry into work, promotion, unemployment, work for both spouses, and biologically for the women the menopause. Another main event is changing of houses. There are, of course, losses, particularly the death of parents, and, later on in life, of friends. These moments and changes demand appropriate response and, although all familiar, they present critical moments of adaptation.

Emotionally the process of growth involves the mastering of all the features that were mentioned as belonging to the immature personality. In marriage the vital element of growth is the development of an awareness of the inner world of one's spouse. We start the intimacy of marriage much better equipped in understanding our own personality and needs. Appreciating that of our partner is the key to a successful relationship. Not only understanding but making sure that we respond accurately to them is vital. This comprehension implies that we are sensitive to their moods, feelings, values, opinions, priorities, and we respect them. Part of the process of change is that all these will alter with time slowly and imperceptibly. Thus, although the central identity of our spouse will remain the same the detail will alter, and sometimes there will be substantial change. We must not take it for granted that our partner always knows themselves even though they have experienced themselves infinitely more deeply than we do. Part of mutual growth is acting like a mirror to each other. We can find out what we are by the way we are responded to by another person. We are also influenced by our partner, and with time we grow more like them.

We can now return to those aspects of growth that happen by degrees. We learn to delay our gratification until that of our partner is met. Mothers will dish out larger portions of food to other members of the family. Both spouses can think of each other's physical needs and supply them. When finances are limited, sacrifices will be made, and the children will come before the adults. We learn to share scarce commodities and to give up things for others. In a family time is rarely one's own and there are the constant demands of spouse and children. All this is the schooling for unselfishness. At the same time we realise that we are needed and appreciated. We sense that we have something to offer and that, however limited our capabilities, we are always trying to offer ourselves.

Such growth does not run smoothly. There is always the temptation to put our own priorities first, but the expectant look of a child or a spouse is a constant reminder that we are there to be available. When the children are young, the end result of constant availability is tiredness, and one of the issues that faces any couple is how to meet the needs of the children without neglecting their own (see Chapter 18).

Delaying gratification, putting ourselves second, being aware of the other and accessible, are all the subjects in the school of loving availability. Each moment becomes a chance for loving.

There is also the dark side of the relationship. The sensitivity to criticism, the conflict of disagreement, the moment of anger and temper outburst. Little by little we become less sensitive, we misunderstand less, we become more resilient, our patience grows, we quarrel less and make up more quickly. We learn to see things from the point of view of our partner and our children. We give in without feeling humiliated and defeated.

Given that our understanding of each other improves, we have to get used to each other's lapses, poor memory, untidiness, or conversely excessive tidiness, the obsession with cleanliness, the limitations of the menu, the many misunderstandings. If the finances are limited, and this applies to many, there is a constant struggle to make ends meet, and when there is financial flexibility some families always manage to live just beyond their resources, with the headaches this involves. It is out of these circumstances that mutual tolerance and understanding grow as the partners make sacrifices for each other and their children. This is the unsung inner world of millions of families.

Coping and adapting results in a mutual growth which leads to a reciprocal respect and appreciation of each other, the hidden basis of love which makes one fond of one's spouse.

There are the general changes and growth processes which proceed all the time. There are, however, some more specific ones.

EMOTIONALLY

Under the category of emotion I want to describe two processes. The reduction of idealisation and the growth from dependence to independence.

As far as idealisation is concerned, we have seen in the period of courtship that there is a heightened awareness of the positive side of our future partner. They appear to excel in intelligence, application, skills, learning, wisdom, sensitivity, and every other quality possible. When we marry, and perhaps nowadays when couples cohabit, they find the reality. The beloved is not so clever or skilled; they are discovered to have problems with changing wheels, gears, opening tins and bottles; are impractical, have no sense of colour, are poor buyers of goods, short in temper, selfish, lazy, untidy, and so on. Spouses have to take deep breaths when faced with the reality. What is more, they have to live with the reality. Despite easy divorce, spouses cannot be exchanged like cars. Idealisation sometimes holds surprises. Partners are found to have hidden talents which were not known. Intimacy unfolds many buds. So the move from idealisation to reality holds both disappointments and positive excitation.

The second process has been mentioned a number of times already. This is the movement from dependence to independence. Men and women can start their relationships by being dependent on each other. They rely on the other for their opinions, initiatives, coping with decision making, handling finances, and so on. With the passage of time confidence is attained, and partners want to take over areas of their lives which they had handed over to their spouse. Spouses can facilitate this growth by encouraging their partner to tackle issues which they have found difficult.

Partnership depends on complementarity. The spouses offer to each other their mutual strengths, but they can also develop additional capacities as they learn from each other.

SEXUALLY

After the initial flush of excitement, sexual activity may become less frequent, but it deepens in quality as the couple discover what pleases each other. Occasionally things go wrong when a wife believes that sex is for children and, when the right number has been achieved, there is no more need for sexual intercourse, but that is rare. Usually there is a deeper appreciation of the sexual dimension as the couple see sex beyond its physical excitement to its supporting effect in their whole life.

PHYSICALLY

The one thing nobody can escape from is the ravages of time. Partners become older and show it by the greying hair, the skin losing its elasticity, and increased weight. It is a measure of love that spouses continue to enjoy each other even in the visible presence of such changes. There can be moments of crisis when a man or a woman enters their forties and become alarmed that they are past the prime of their life. This is where loving reassurance comes into play, and they are reminded that they matter for themselves.

Another factor that may make a sudden and unexpected entry is illness. This may strike at any age, even though the majority of couples will not experience it until late in their married life. Sometimes such conditions as disseminated sclerosis or rheumatic diseases, cancer, may occur early. Part of mature growth is coping with such adversity.

INTELLIGENCE AND CREATIVITY

Like our physical development, our intelligence has reached its final form before we enter marriage. Our IQ will not suddenly rise. But if our general intelligence is fixed, our capacity to move from intelligence to wisdom is considerable. We learn from many people and many sources but our most constant mentor is our spouse who has regular access to us. They can be our most constructive critics and help us refine our intelligence to unexpected heights.

This facilitation extends into the support we receive when we want to try a new venture at any stage in our life. The new venture can be cooking, gardening, engaging in any new activity and even changing the course of our life by trying a new job. We need imagination and opportunity, but above all encouragement and facilitation to develop hidden talents.

Change and growth are visible over time, but hard to detect day by day. In fact every moment of a life together is an opportunity to facilitate the other person, whatever they need. There is tension between self-awareness and the development of one's own needs, and the sensitive awareness and respect of our partner's needs. The usual explanation is that we are all selfish, and the only battle in life is to defeat selfishness. Psychology has shown us that selfishness can be re-interpreted by understanding ourselves, particularly our anxieties and fears which make us protective of ourselves so that we appear selfish, and the sensitive awareness of the inner world of the other which is then facilitated. Married life is about change which enhances personal growth from immaturity to maturity, dependence to independence, idealisation to reality, and facilitates the partner to engage in the same process. It takes a lifetime to get to know each other and respond accurately, but in the process, in the Christian sense, we are developing the qualities of the Trinity, in which three persons know each other perfectly and respond to each other fully. The growth of marital love is about this process and it takes a long time to achieve it. The essential accompaniments are continuity, reliability and predictability, which have been shown repeatedly to be necessary for marital love, and are

good reasons why marriage needs to be permanent if it is
going to fulfil its potential.

11

Sexual Love

Sexuality, the central dynamic energy between men and women, has had a poor history in Christianity. The reasons are multiple, but three principal ones exist. The first was Greek and Stoic philosophy which played its part. With this tradition there was a prediliction for ataraxia, which is a special freedom of the mind from the passions. Sexual arousal and the climax of intercourse were certainly emotionally agitating experiences. The orgasm was considered to show a loss of control of reason, and at that moment human sexual activity was equated with the animal kingdom. This disparaging view of sex as animal instinct was to have a long and profound influence on Christian theology. The loss of control was considered to be profoundly damaging to human dignity, and the man who controlled his passions was definitely a superior being.

The second element was the presence of surrounding religions with strong elements of Gnosticism and Manicheism. These were complicated religions, but central to them was the belief that the physical, the Body and the flesh, trapped this spirit and the soul, and that sexual intercourse with its procreative potential was an enemy of the spirit. Marriage and sex should be avoided. Christianity was confronted with the task of protecting marriage and yet distancing itself from sexual intercourse, although it had to testify that new life was good and to be protected in the womb. Hence abortion was considered to be gravely wrong.

The third element was the opinion of individual Greek and Latin Fathers. Among the latter St Augustine turned out to be most influential. In his youth Augustine had known powerful sexual passion. He said to God, 'Give me chastity – but not yet.' There is little doubt that this strong sexual appetite played an important role in his later deliberations. He wrote on marriage, which he held to be good, and he laid down the three goods of marriage as *proles, fides, sacramentum*; or children, mutual faithfulness, and indissolubility of the union. These three concepts, which in the Middle Ages became the ends of marriage, had a powerful and enduring impact on the theology of the Catholic Church. But as far as sexual intercourse is concerned, he took a pessimistic view, holding that it was always at least venially sinful, and that its only justification was the procreation of children. There was no association with love, and this genius set western theology on a false track in this area with repercussions that we still see today, for sexuality became inextricably linked with biology and not love. This was an anomaly in a saint who recognised and wrote extensively about the supreme importance of love.

Later in the Middle Ages theologians, like Aquinas, modified Augustine's view on sexual passion, and indeed formulated the position that a deliberate, intended, and anticipated enjoyment of sex was right and proper. The essential link between sex and procreation, however, was maintained. This conjunction was necessary because it had a ring of truth about it. There was no status accorded to women and their inner world, and no connection was made with human love. Attempts were made sporadically in the Middle Ages to link love with sex, but they did not grip formal theology, although we do not know in detail how married people experienced sex. We know in the case of Abélard and Héloïse that a strong emotional attachment was to be found in their relationship.

It was only in our day that the link between love and sex was finally recognised in the Second Vatican Council, although preceding encyclicals had seen the importance of love in marriage. The expression of love in sex needs elaboration, and an attempt will be made in this chapter to do this.

The link between sex and love is urgently needed because the presence of widespread contraception and the accuracy of pregnancy with birth regulation has meant that the overwhelming majority of sexual acts are no longer procreative.

Both society and the Church need to find a new meaning for sexual intercourse. A few sexual acts are all that are needed to have the present size family. In the absence of an alternative meaning, hedonism is running rampant all over the world, and yet, as we shall see, there are alternative meanings.

SEXUAL INTERCOURSE

From the time of puberty, sexual arousal and attraction is designed for the sexual act. The sexes approach sexual arousal differently. For both, the hormone testosterone is related to sexual drive. Both men and women are aroused sexually and want to have sex, but common observation and studies show a physical urgency in men, not to be found in women. In fact the sexuality of men is marked by physicality, and that of women by affectionality. This is something that couples have to learn about each other. The man is aroused by vision, sound and touch connected with the erotic, and up to a point women are also excited, but for the latter the atmosphere of the relationship counts a great deal. The quality of the relationship matters to women, for whom the preceding hours before sex need to be affectionate and warm. So women have to accustom themselves to the physical sexual urgency of men, and men have to learn that atmosphere is important to their wives, although, of course, there are exceptions from these generalities. In so far as they hold true, it is part of the loving of the couple that they should take notice of each other's needs and try to meet them.

This challenge of love extends to the preparation for making love. Men have the urgency which drives them to make genital contact with the greatest speed. Women may be spontaneously aroused, but often need to be caressed, stroked, hugged, kissed and erotically excited. Here loving requires control and patience on the part of the man, and a willingness to participate in sex by the wife when she has no special desire for it. Love is now shown in control and patience on the part of the man, and a generosity on the part of the woman, rather than compliant or resigned sex.

91

The same patience applies to the actual sexual intercourse itself when the man has to hold back his climax in order to ensure that his wife reaches her orgasm too. This is a loving consideration in the very midst of the act itself. Traditional morality was concerned with the position that the couple adopted to have coitus. One can say categorically that a couple can adopt any position which mutually satisfies them, and give to each other any erotic excitation that is pleasurable.

During the preparation for sex and the act itself, the couple may find themselves fantasising about each other or about erotic scenes which are usually impersonal. This intrusion of fantasies may be highly erotic, but men and women may worry deep down whether such fantasies are legitimate, and fear that in the end they may betray their partner. We do not understand the psychology of such fantasies, which at their extreme may be sado-masochistic or have other fetishist connotations. It may be considered whether morality should have any say at such intensely private moments. The whole point of sexual intercourse is to experience and give erotic pleasure. The more personal and spouse-orientated it is the better, but at the moment the whole sexual array of individual fantasy is aroused and it cannot be easily controlled. It has to be accepted that the range of arousal, whatever its nature, is moral, provided it leads to mutually pleasurable experiences.

Throughout this book constant references are made to love having its beginning in the world of infancy and childhood. The adult sexual act appears on the surface to have no connection with that era, but this is not the case. In the process of the genital interaction the two bodies make an intimate, secure, close, rhythmic contact which has a strong reminder of the intimate closeness between baby and mother with the same rhythm of intimacy. In fact this smooth two-in-one unity is at its best when the couple are relaxed and enjoying sex. When one or the other is alienated, they become tense, unrelaxed and withdrawn bodily and genitally from each other and, although having sex, they are functioning as separate persons.

The conclusion of the act is to be found in the orgasm,

which for the man almost invariably leads to exquisite pleasure accompanied by rhythmic spasm of the penis with ejection of sperm. The woman may enjoy a similar orgasmic sensation, but she may not always do so. Part of loving in these circumstances is for the husband manually to give her an orgasm and release the accumulated sexual tension. Whatever the method, the object of the exercise is for the couple to reach mutual orgasm with its exquisite pleasure and joy.

Sexual intercourse is not always the highly exciting experience that it is meant to be. One or the other spouse may be tired, disinterested sexually, not relaxed enough, or may be submitting reluctantly to the act. For a variety of reasons, the personal closeness may be absent and the act becomes a physical one only. For complete unity, the act should combine the personal component of mutual surrender and joy in each other, accompanied by the physical infrastructure. The two do not always combine, and sometimes there is just a release of sexual tension, while occasionally there is not even that. Some women have rarely enjoyed sex, particularly in previous generations when sex was strongly confined to having a child. So while sex can be ecstatic, it can also become routine, and occasionally boring. Every effort should be made to guard it against banality, and try to make it something special because it is a symbol of the whole meaning of the encounter between spouses.

THE MEANING OF SEXUAL INTERCOURSE

Earlier in this chapter I referred to the contemporary challenge of discovering the meaning of sexual intercourse when it is carried out for forty or fifty years after the desired family size has been attained.

The first thing to say is that the evolution of the human species has made sexual intercourse the means of perpetuating the race. There is a biological basis to sex, which at the very heart is a release from sexual tension fuelled by hormones. We would be ignoring the animal side of men and women if we failed to acknowledge the basic physical dimension. But everything we know points to the fact that there is more to humanity than being high animals. There is a clear indication of the presence of the spirit and in the context of the Christian faith, the revelation about God, and our eternal destiny with him.

So we must move on to the more personal dimension which does justice to the sexual domain. As mentioned already, the loving dimensions of sustaining, healing and growth need constant nurturing. It is not easy to be available, to communicate effectively, to show affection, and to negotiate conflict without a constant supply of energy and encouragement which sexual intercourse gives and which also rewards the efforts made. The same applies to healing and growth. Responding to the wounded part of our partner is often dealing with the irritable, angry, impatient, impulsive, intolerant, generally difficult part of our spouse. This requires patience, persistence, and motivation which are supplied by sexual intercourse as well as the reward for the sustained effort.

In thinking about the personal meaning of sexual intercourse, I have for some time described five individual characteristics which seem to be standing the test of time, and so I am repeating them here. These are features which are not consciously experienced, but are the existential reality of coitus, which are nevertheless immensely rich in their personal implications. Generally what I am trying to convey in these five features is the sense that sexual intercourse is a body language of love in which the couple are talking to each other with their bodies. What are they saying to each other?

The first communication is the acknowledgement that in allowing each other access to themselves sexually they are saying to each other 'I recognise, want and appreciate you. You are the most important person in my life'. In this context sexual intercourse is a powerful affirmation of personhood.

Secondly, when the sexual act is performed in a fulfilling manner, the man is able to make the woman feel completely feminine and the woman can make the man most completely masculine. It is a way that human sexuality is brought to life. In this way the couple affirm the sexual identity of each other.

Thirdly, mention has been made already of the fact that

94

the couple will experience conflict, anger and pain from each other. Most hurts are quickly forgotten and forgiven, but some go deeper and the pain can be excruciating. There is much evidence that after hours, days or weeks in pain, it is sexual intercourse that brings reconciliation. So its third feature is that it can act as a reconciliatory, healing language.

Fourthly, all human beings are overtly seeking meaning in our lives. We do not often spend time speculating where we come from, the meaning of life and where we are going. In the depths of our faith we seek the meaning, but we long for an answer. The knowledge that at regular intervals another human being wants you and is prepared to celebrate life through sexual intercourse is a repeated act of profound meaning in life. It is therefore an act of recurrent hope.

Finally, as human beings we need to render thanks for our life. Sexual intercourse is the act through which we say thank you for being with me yesterday, today, and I hope tomorrow. It is a recurrent act of thanksgiving.

While still staying with sexual intercourse we can speculate about the meaning of the act in a strictly spiritual sense by referring to the Trinity. The mystery of the Trinity is beyond comprehension, but it implies a total unity of three persons while they remain completely separate and unique in themselves. Attempts have been made to allocate roles to each person, such as creativity, love and wisdom. But in the sexual act we might have a model of the total unity of two persons while each retains their complete separate identity. We should not forget that Paul describes the loving unity and relationship of Christ and the Church in terms of marriage and the marital act. Thus sexual intercourse is the central and recurrent act of prayer of the couple.

CHILDREN

In all this some may observe that in the midst of this personal expression of love the idea of children seems to be lost, and the whole tradition which has been the infrastructure of Christianity disappears at a stroke.

Those who resisted the dropping of the traditional language in the Second Vatican Council of primary and secondary ends in which the primary end was the procreation and education of children, may remind us that they had good reason to be anxious.

Traditionalists repeat that the Second Vatican Council said:

> Hence, while not making the other purposes of matrimony of less account, the true practice of conjugal love, and the whole meaning of family life which results from it, have this aim; that the couple be ready with stout hearts to co-operate with the love of the Creator and the Saviour, who through them will enlarge and enrich his own family day by day.
>
> (Pastoral Constitution, Part 2, ch. 1)

There are several observations to be made on this topic. First of all, everyone should be reminded that the council removed the language of primary and second ends. Secondly the personal meaning of sexual intercourse goes on, whether the couple are opening their sexual act to new life or not. What couples experience in the act is its personal meaning, not the possible fusion between sperm and ovum, however much they may want a baby. Most important of all, however, is the reality that everything we have learned about children tells us that they need security and love, and that depends on the stability of the couple and their capacity to be loving parents. This viability of the couple and the whole welfare of the children depends on the support that sexual intercourse gives to the parents. To stress the biology of sex is to ignore the personal which is its supreme value, and, even more important, to forget that after the family has been completed there may be several decades when sexual intercourse continues. The trouble with Christian teaching in the past is that by stressing the biological it has trivialised the act. Everyone knows that sex is needed for children, and that will always remain. It is the personal that needs stressing.

MORALITY OF SEX

It can be seen from what has been said that there is a personal morality within marriage invested in sexual intercourse. One can be unloving in marriage when one takes one's partner for granted, ceases to take the trouble to make love, and instead one has sex.

Sex outside marriage was traditionally forbidden because a child might be conceived without the presence of loving parents. The advent of widespread contraception no longer motivates people in this way, although plenty of mistakes are made which often lead to abortion.

Bringing a life into the world without two parents is a grave mistake and highly irresponsible. Even more important, in the light of what has been said in this chapter, is the fact that sexual intercourse contains some of the deepest, personal and loving experiences of life, and its authentic meaning can only be experienced within the context of a continuous, reliable and predictable relationship which is usually marriage. Making love is a powerful evocation of what true love is, and the authenticity is highly traumatised when it is trivialised through promiscuity. The ultimate denial of its meaning is in the union of the prostitute and her client when bodies meet without a personal encounter, and therefore with the total absence of love.

But while the prostitute and her client share the crumbs of comfort of monetary exchange and the residue of sexual pleasure, sexual difficulties exist for many couples who are trying to make authentic love. These problems will be described in Part II.

Part II

*Marital Problems and the
Response to Them*

12

Marital Difficulties

Marital difficulties are a normal accompaniment of the intimacy of contemporary marriage. Traditionally the man was considered the head of the family, and the wife was expected to obey him. If she did not like the way things were, a large part of tradition dictated that she had to adapt to them. In practice women resisted, defied and used their considerable emotional and sexual powers to rectify the situation, but in theory the man was considered to be in charge.

Today there is an increasing equality between the sexes, and differences are meant to be sorted out by negotiation. This works out in many marriages, but not in all. There are spouses who cannot accept that their actions are intolerable, and they persist with them. Many others see that change is needed but unsatisfactory habits continue and the pattern of behaviour which is annoying does not alter. There may be rows and promises, but nothing is done, and so resentment and anger build up.

The difficulties which couples encounter may appear innumerable, but in practice the common ones can be identified and dealt with. The problems can be divided into those of the quality of the relationship and specific problems.

Looking at the quality of the relationship, the model which is used has been devised by the author and consists of two sets of ideas. The first is that the marriage relationship has five main dimensions: the social, emotional, sexual, intellectual and spiritual. When the couple come together they engage along a wide front on all these five areas, any one of which may present difficulties. The second idea is that marriage proceeds by phases. These can cover the period before

101

childbearing, the phase in which the first child is between the ages of one and five, when it enters school, when all the children are at primary school, when the eldest is in secondary school, when all are in secondary school, when the eldest leaves school, when all leave school, and finally leave home. Then the couple return to their twosome state which may last twenty years or more. Each of these stages has its own challenge, which, as we have seen, comprise the maintenance of the parents' relationship and the parenting role.

For the sake of brevity these phases have been reduced to three in the model used here. Phase one covers the first five years, which usually brings the couple to the age of thirty. This is the period when usually the children arrive, and the mother ceases work. There is a new adaptation with the mother taking a new role and the father becoming provider for the whole family.

The second phase is between the ages of thirty and fifty. This is the period when the children are growing up, frequently the mother returns to work, and the mid-life crisis occurs, ending with the menopause for the wife. By the end of this phase the children have usually left home. These are the toughest years of marriage, combining the main responsibilities of bringing up the children with change in the outlook of the spouses. Change is the key word to describe this phase.

The third phase is between the age of fifty and the death of one spouse. This is the period when the couple return to their one-to-one state, they become a dyad once again. The children have usually left home without necessarily interrupting their constant need for advice, money and contact. The extended family brings grandparents, children and grandchildren together.

The description of the common problems does not usually tell us how to solve them. Conflicts occur all the time in marriage. The first thing to do is to try to evaluate the significance of what is happening. We need to distinguish between the hurts we experience at the hands of our spouses through poor memory, inattention, lapse of good manners, untidiness, impulsiveness, transient anger, which are quickly forgotten, and the dissatisfaction which affects the very core

102

of one's being. In the latter case, we may discover that our integrity is being damaged by the restriction of our freedom, the neglect of being loved, the lack of realisation of our potential, the unwarranted attacks on our wellbeing. In other words, an essential part of our humanity is in danger.

Here is an important factor from the Christian point of view. When we are married, are we expected to suffer all kinds of indignities and humiliations in order to stay married? This is a point of view that fundamental Christian circles take. For them the state of marriage is permanent, and nothing ever excuses a divorce. The Roman Catholic Church takes a very strict view on indissolubility, but nevertheless grants annulments. Consideration will be given to this later on, but in the meantime it is worth noting what Canon Law has to say on the subject.

Canon 1095 of the new Canon Law states:

The following are incapable of contracting marriage:

1 Those who lack sufficient use of reason.
2 Those who suffer from a grave lack of discretionary judgment concerning the essential matrimonial rights and obligations to be mutually given and accepted.
3 Those who, because of causes of a psychological nature, are unable to assume the essential obligations of marriage.

What are the essential obligations of marriage? Canon 1055 states:

The Marriage covenant, by which a man and a woman establish between themselves a partnership of their whole life, and which of its own very nature is ordered to the well-being of the spouses and to the procreation and upbringing of children has, between the baptised, been raised by Christ the Lord to the dignity of a Sacrament.

The point to be taken from this Canon is that the nature of marriage is ordered to 'the well-being of the spouses', which, as we have seen in the documents of the Second Vatican Council, is orientated towards love.

In other words, the spouses are entitled to look at whether their essential needs of love are being met. There are, of course, differences between what the secular world considers the essentials of love, and what the Church accepts, but there is a convergence that the essentials of love have to be safeguarded.

This is the clue to the way marital difficulties have to be evaluated. Is the conflict involving something essential to the concept of love for the spouse, or something inessential? Clearly it takes time for the spouse to appreciate that a persistent problem exists which appears recurrent and unchangeable. When that moment of realisation has arrived, when something fundamental is missing or is wrong with the relationship, what should the spouse do? This is the moment of truth. Everything should be done to challenge the partner about the issue. They should repeatedly be faced with it, asked to change, cajoled, if necessary bullied and threatened. When the issue is vital, there should be no let up in the persuasion, and this includes the assistance to change. If still no change takes place, the spouse should ask themselves whether they should seek counselling help. Taking the matter outside the home is an indication of seriousness which sometimes makes the partner face issues which they adamantly refused to look at before. If there is still no resolution to the problem, then they should consider whether they are prepared to accept the limitation and stay, or decide to depart.

What usually happens is that spouses remain frustrated and dissatisfied for years without taking decisive action to confront their partner. Then one day they simply pack their bags and go. It is necessary, when a serious defect is diagnosed, that the spouse should be confronted, and it is with this in mind that the next three chapters are written.

13

Marital Difficulties – First Phase

The first five years of marriage constitute in this model the first phase of marriage. These years are significant in three ways. They are the important years of adjustment, and they are loaded with difficulties. Secondly, it has been found that they are very important in laying the foundations of the welfare of the relationship. Whenever a marriage breaks down, people put the causes in these early years. Thirdly, it has been found that between 30 per cent and 40 per cent of all marital breakdown occurs in these first five years. So they are important and they should be supported. Let us consider the five dimensions in this phase.

SOCIAL FACTORS

Separation from parents

At the centre of marriage lies the separation of the spouses from the parents and the fusion of a new unity between husband and wife. The parents remain important, are contacted and resorted to. They remain good friends. But the spouses turn to each other for the resolution of their difficulties, the management of their affairs, the future planning and the timing of children. It is natural that in all these matters they should consult each other and take mutual decisions, leaving the parents out of the consideration.

This happens with the majority of couples, but there are exceptions and they produce the problems. In these instances, one or both spouses remain over-attached to the parents. The wife may be over-dependent on the mother, and the husband on the father. The girl telephones her mother several times a day, or visits her at frequent intervals. The mother becomes the confidante of the daughter. The vital secrets of the relationship are entrusted to her. Instead of discussing matters with her husband, she communicates with her mother and the husband is bypassed. His opinions are ignored in favour of the parents'. The husband turns to the father for advice on economic matters and, worse still, may be employed by the father who expects to exert a dominant part in the life of his son. Just as the daughter bypasses the husband, he bypasses her. In this way the couple are married but they have not left the dependence on their families.

This is a situation which leads to the partners feeling excluded and not treated as a proper spouse. Repeated requests to abandon the dependence on the parent are ignored. The next phase of this problem is that the spouse is criticised, and an alliance is formed between parent and the child against the spouse. The situation gets much worse with the formation of triangular tensions between parents and the partners. In the end the marriage may come to an end.

The more common problem is when a spouse is not liked or approved of by his family-in-law. This puts the other partner in difficulties. They have to choose between their spouse and their parent which leads to classical rows.

Running the household

When a couple are newly married they have to make arrangements for running the home. Traditionally the wife has assumed responsibility for the domestic side, and the husband the practical, mechanical aspects and those that require heavy lifting. Nowadays there is much more fluidity of roles, and the husbands cook and do other domestic chores.

The important thing is that the distribution should be fair and experienced as such. What may happen is that the wife is lumbered with all the household chores, work, and in due course looking after the children. The husband may consider it sufficient to be a provider and do next to nothing in the home. This leads to a common problem which is that of excessive tiredness on the part of the wife, and tiredness is a killer of affection and sex.

One of the complications is that during the courtship the man may promise the moon, and then, when it comes to the actual marriage, fail to deliver. Here is the added frustration of disappointment, and the feeling of being let down.

Money

If one listens to a cross-section of opinion, the most common explanation offered for marriage troubles is finance, inadequate money. Money is meant to solve all the problems. The fact that no mention of it has been made up till now is because, while money undoubtedly matters, it is the emotional consequences that are responsible for the conflict. There are plenty of poor people who maintain their marriage, and the rich whose marriages do not work. We have to look at the meaning of money and see the implications.

Money has three meanings – the first is its economic entity, the second denotes power for the hands that hold it, the third has an emotional component.

The first element is the one that is usually considered. This often means that there is not enough of it. Since money is essential to purchase a house, food, clothing, and other essentials of life, then its relative absence leads to tension, quarrels, arguments and mutual accusations.

The person who holds the purse has power over their partner. It is the husband who usually holds the money, and traditionally the wife has been dependent on him for her financial survival. If he does not give her enough money for the necessities, she is unable to do anything about it except to go to work herself, and then she very often uses the money she earns to supplement the household budget.

In certain marriages the wife marries only to discover that the husband cannot handle the money and is irresponsible with it. He squanders it, drinks in excess, and gambles it away. This is an enormous strain on the young couple.

107

Thirdly, money has an emotional meaning. The woman who is kept short of money feels unloved. She thinks to herself, 'If you loved me, you would not keep me short.'

Housing

A young couple newly married want a place of their own. When they have to share with their families, or with other people, the scene is set for strain, and it has been found that those who start married life without an independent abode have a greater tendency towards marital breakdown.

Work

Work is important in the life of the couple for its economic value, social support and their self-esteem. There are two problems which are associated with it. These are working excessive hours, and unemployment.

Anyone can work long hours, but it is a problem which particularly affects professional people. The doctor, solicitor, accountant, all work long hours and come home late. This leads to constant arguments that they put their work before their spouse. When they come home they are tired and unavailable for conversation. Very often they have their meal, sit in front of the television and fall asleep. This is usually exceedingly tiresome to the wife.

The other problem is that professional people have to travel abroad and leave their spouse behind. When this is frequent it can create an emotional vacuum which is acutely painful.

Another problem is unemployment. Unemployment has a devastating effect on self-esteem, and the feelings of emotional availability, particularly for the man. It is not surprising that it is associated with a high rate of marital breakdown.

Leisure

One of the dangers in the early years of marriage is that the spouse, often the husband, will want to enjoy the amenities of marriage, an organised household, needing food and sex, while he uses his spare time to continue his favourite leisure, be it sport or spending time with his friends in the pub. The pub in particular can be a sort of substitute home, and time spent there can be really offensive to the wife.

EMOTIONAL

The emotional factors have been mentioned before in various parts of this book. Here they will be briefly collated.

Loss of idealisation

It has been shown that what holds a couple together in the stage of falling in love is their deep idealisation of each other. In brief they think they are wonderful. Those who are wise begin to accept, even at this stage, that there are limitations to the partner. The limitations are social, as described above, or emotional, that is, in the language already used, they have shortcomings in their emotional availability, capacity to feel, be affectionate or understanding. When they are foreseen, there is damage limitation. When they strike unexpectedly in the early years, there is acute disappointment – 'this is not the man/woman I fell in love with. I can't recognise them. They have changed so.' Such sentences herald profound disillusionment.

Restriction of freedom

In some instances the newly married person cannot cope with the limitations imposed on their freedom of movement and/or action. Such a person suddenly feels imprisoned, and within months of the marriage is desperately unhappy and wants to be out of it. When close attention is paid to the period of the courtship and the previous history, it will be found that he or she may have broken off the relationship more than once or been involved with previous courtships which they could not negotiate. In fact, such men or women may postpone the marriage repeatedly beforehand and once they are in it find it intolerable. Within the marriage, they become depressed and withdrawn, and all they want is to get out.

Inability to cope with intimacy

The inability to cope with intimacy is another side of the few vulnerable people who marry and then regret it immediately afterwards. They form the extreme pattern of avoidant attachment, and cannot stand any form of closeness. They made the supreme effort to overcome their difficulty during courtship, but the continuous physical and emotional closeness is intolerable.

Immaturity

The man or woman who after marriage displays the behaviour of immaturity may come as a shock to their partner. There may have been indications during the courtship, but they were not interpreted correctly. The behaviour consists of one or more symptoms of recurrent and acute loss of temper, excessive drinking, aggression with physical and verbal assault, inconsistent and poor work record, sexual excess, rudeness and possessiveness. Clearly such behaviour is inconsistent with the continuation of the marriage, and is a massive expression of immaturity.

SEXUAL

Non-consummation

This is a functional disturbance in which the wife finds penetration impossible. It is perfectly capable of being corrected.

Birth regulation

Most couples do not have any difficulty with birth regulation. They use the method most suited to them. If one spouse is a Roman Catholic, he or she may want to restrict birth regulation to the methods acceptable to their Church. There is no difficulty in finding suitable training programmes to accommodate this special need.

Poor loving

The disappointment with sexual intercourse in the first five years of marriage is unlikely to involve major functional disorders in the male, but may do so in the woman. She may not reach orgasm and/or may experience pain during intercourse.

More commonly there may be disappointment in the quality of lovemaking. One of the couple may feel that sex is not as rewarding as it was during courtship and not so frequent. The man may complain about frequency, and the woman about the ambience of the lovemaking.

Difficulty in getting pregnant

A small percentage of couples, of the order of 8 per cent, do not become pregnant when they want to. This leads to the ordeal of investigations, keeping charts, taking the fertility pill, and even proceeding to in vitro fertilisation. The couple may understand with their head that it is not their fault, but they feel embarrassed about their difficulty. The husband may be found to have a low sperm count which is a blow to his self-esteem, and the wife may have hormonal difficulties. This is a time when the spontaneity of sexual intercourse is reduced and the spouses become mechanically involved in the challenge of reproduction. Their desire to become fertile is intermingled with the disappointment and frustration of not being able to become so. This is a testing time, and the couple need encouragement to get over the difficulties.

Sexual variations

Some partners want to embroider sexual intercourse with some extra-sexual activity, such as a fetish, cross-dressing or sado-masochistic practices. The wife, who is the recipient of such desires, may feel the request surprising or upsetting. She

111

should seek help to aid her to understand her husband's needs.

Occasionally a homosexual man or woman marries to 'cure' their homosexuality, or to prove to themselves that they are not saddled with this difficulty. To their surprise they find they cannot continue with the marriage, and to the dismay of their partner give up. Although such an event is exceedingly painful, it is better if faced early in the marriage than later on.

Affairs

The early years of marriage are not usually a time when infidelity occurs. Sometimes it does. The affair may involve an ex-girlfriend or ex-boyfriend, and may be the remnants of an unresolved relationship. As with all affairs, the pain should not stop the process of reconciliation.

INTELLECTUAL

A couple would usually test each other for common interests, outlook, opinion, in the process of the courtship or cohabitation. There they will find out whether they have a common background, their educational outlook coincides, and they can interest one another apart from in bed. Occasionally a hasty courtship, or one based on infatuation, brings partners together who have little in common. This combination of bodies and not of minds was common in previous generations, and it still happens occasionally.

When it does happen, there has to be an assessment whether there is a sufficiency of intellectual affinity to keep the spouses together.

SPIRITUALITY

The same applies to the spiritual dimension. The number of people who share the same faith varies from country to

112

country. In Ireland there will be a high rate of similar Roman Catholic backgrounds. In Britain there will be a similar incidence of Protestant faiths. The Roman Catholic community in Britain is increasingly marrying outside its own faith, and this may pose in some instances issues with birth regulation. But generally few partners interfere with the practice of the faith of their spouse, or the upbringing of their children in the religion desired by the partner who, in the case of the Roman Catholic parent, will choose that faith.

Occasionally the faith or values of the couple clash, and there may be conflict, but this is rare.

14

Marital Difficulties –
Second Phase

The second phase of marriage progresses from the age of thirty to fifty. It comprises the years when the children are growing up, the wife may return to work, the husband climbs the ladder of success, remains stuck at a certain level, or slides downwards. Above all it is characterised by change of awareness and personality which is fundamental to the survival of the marriage. The major part of marital breakdown occurs during these years, and the challenges of maintaining the relationship are most acute during this time.

SOCIAL

Work

At the centre of these years is the work performance of the spouses, particularly the husband, although increasingly the wife's career matters. The husband may rise steadily up the professional ladder, and this may present problems. The difficulties may arise from being promoted to a level which is aspired to, but is beyond the capabilities of the individual. This may produce a situation in which the husband is under stress with accompanying symptoms of poor sleep, irritability, angry outbursts, inability to relax, and finally a mood of depression with apathy, tiredness, lack of energy, and even tears. These men are exhausted and cannot cope at home or at work. Having reached the pinnacle of their achievement, they find it very difficult to recognise that they cannot handle

114

its demands. They have nowhere to go and they vent their tension on their wife and children. They may come to marriage counselling, thinking that there is something wrong with their relationship when in fact their marriage is suffering the strain of work. In these circumstances illness may be a way out. The doctor may offer an acceptable excuse to abandon the work undertaken, and to take on something more suitable.

Closely associated with promotion difficulties is the burned out individual who exhibits all the same symptoms of strain. After years in the same job, such a person becomes drained of ideas, energy, innovation, and a sense of despair covers all his activities. There is no point in carrying on, with frustration and irritability taking over. This burned out syndrome, which may be complicated by depression, invades the family and sours relationships. A prolonged holiday, change in work, the addition of hobbies, or even early retirement, are useful ploys in coping with the situation.

At the other end of the scale will be found unemployment. Unemployment can affect every social scale, from senior executives to manual workers, and they all respond with shock, seeing it as an attack on their self-esteem. In particular the person who lacks confidence from their personal relationships and relies on work for it, finds unemployment especially hard to take. If their self-esteem emanated from their work, then at a stroke they are rendered impotent as people. Their power basis evaporates, and the single most important reason for existing disappears. In their own eyes they become worthless because their position, status and money was the passport to their identity. Now they have lost their sense of direction, and, without work, feel rudderless. They find it difficult to recognise any remaining value in themselves, and they withdraw in a state of anger, resentment, despair or futility. In this heightened plight of irritability they pick quarrels, turn to drink, fail to look after themselves or their family, feel sad or distressed, and cannot take the initiative. There is good evidence that unemployment increases the incidence of marital breakdown.

The wife of an unemployed person needs to remind him that he still matters to her independently of the lack of work.

This is a hard task which has to be expressed in affection, sex, encouragement and reassurance. In the household there has to be a balance between finding tasks for him to do and not insulting him by appearing to turn him into an enfeebled and emasculated individual. Keeping up hope of re-employment is vital, even if there is a diminished opportunity for it. Above all, allowances have to be made for his sensitivity and inability to respond in a relaxed manner.

During these years men and women find themselves in a position of uncertainty about their future. They may not be advancing or receding, but standing still, uncertain where to go next. Such indetermination may lead them to put pressure on their spouse to make up their minds. The partner should refuse this. The choice of staying, leaving or changing careers is something which only the individual should decide. The best thing the spouse can do is to help their partner evaluate the situation. Are they doing what they want to do in their present job? Are they being fulfilled? Are they realising their potential? Are they rightly or wrongly resentful at the way they are being treated? These and similar questions should be considered together, but the final decision regarding future choice should be placed squarely on the shoulders of the person whose life is involved.

Children

These twenty years cover the period when the children are growing up. From about the age of seven or eight young people will challenge the authority of the parents. They will want to know why the parents are asking or demanding certain behaviour, and they will judge it according to the criterion of fairness. The whole sense of justice and fairness will begin to arise from this age onwards. Parents cannot get away with naked authority, and they have to justify their demands and behaviour. Children are outraged if they feel their parents are behaving in an authoritarian way.

As puberty breaks through, the incest taboo prevails. Boys will resist being cuddled and loved by their mother, and girls will flirt with father. There is a need to treat the adolescent

116

as an adult in miniature, both emotionally and sexually. This is the time when parents will be absorbed with the responsibility of protecting their children from the dangers of too much freedom socially, emotionally and sexually. If they are not careful, they will be divided in their expectations, and these years can become tense for the spouses. The adolescent is one moment behaving like an adult, and the next as a child, and this confuses the parents. The father may incline towards harsh discipline, and the mother towards softness. The anxieties of the spouses may be projected on each other, and lead to quarrels about the best way of controlling the situation. Smoking, drinking, dress, staying out late, school work, may all become issues needing a combined approach, in which the parents are seen to think and act together.

Housing

Change of house may occur once, or more often, during these years. Moving house is highly traumatic. Leaving one's relatives, friends, church, doctor, is painful and is a source of grief. This pain may afflict the wife more than the husband, whose prime source of emotional meaning is work. The trauma of changing house may become stress experienced by the couple, and particularly if one of them did not want to move. Even if there is no conflict, it is important that the period of the change-over is surrounded by a heightened awareness of the accompanying stress, and the couple are ready to support one another.

EMOTIONAL

From dependence to independence

One of the major shifts during these years has already been mentioned, but it bears repeating several times because it is crucial to contemporary marriage. This is the movement from emotional dependence to independence. A couple start life with the wife being dependent on her husband, although it

117

may happen the other way round. The wife relies on her husband for her opinions, values, ideas, initiatives and behaviour. She depends on him to drive her around, handle the finances, decide on houses, holidays and the other important matters in her life. This pattern goes on for a number of years, and then imperceptibly the wife begins to find her confidence through her children, work, or some assertive training.

What follows is vital for the marriage. In one marriage the husband begins to see the change, rejoices and encourages it. He helps his wife to make up her mind, take the initiative, learn to drive, handle the finances, and express her own singular views. This move from dependence to independence proceeds smoothly and advantageously for both partners. The alternative is for the husband to see his wife's growth as a threat to his position. Instead of welcoming her initiatives, he blocks them. To her desire to learn to drive he says, 'I have always driven you around. Why do you want to drive? Am I not good enough? In any case, we can't afford two cars, and women drivers are bad drivers.' To her plea to handle some of the finances, he puts her down by saying, 'I have always done that, taken care, good care, of you. Why do you want to bother your *little* head with such things?' Every effort on her part to take over is frustrated by him. This makes her angry, and she begins to challenge him, do her own thing, and refuse to submit to his will. There are ensuing quarrels, and arguments, and when he comes for counselling he says he does not recognise the girl he married. This inability to facilitate her development expresses his own insecurity which compels him to control everybody around him. As she becomes more independent, he begins to be frightened of losing her. He asks her for reassurance that she still loves him, which she refuses to give, both because she is angry and because she is not sure that she does love him. The husband is under stress with tension, torn between his anxiety, his fear that he is losing his grip on the situation, and his confusion about what to do. Counselling can help to explain what is going on in the relationship, and what changes are needed. If the changes do not take place, then the wife may look elsewhere for a man who appreciates her growing talents and initiatives, and accepts her unconditionally as he finds her.

From insecurity to security

A number of spouses start their relationship with the anxiety of being abandoned, and the fear of authority. The fear of being abandoned is deeply ingrained in their attachment behaviour. They expect to be abandoned for no obvious reason, or they feel unlovable and unwanted. This fear leads them to behave in an appeasing manner, giving in to all the whims of their spouse. If the spouse is emotionally and sexually demanding, then their partner will give in and try to please them, even if this puts them under constant strain. They work on the principle: 'I know I am not good enough for you, and you may give me up at any moment. I can never succeed in pleasing you completely, but I will do all I can to satisfy you. If I go on pleasing you, then you may decide not to abandon me.' This insecurity, like dependence, may change with time. The spouse may find their own security through success in their own life or through an affair which makes them feel wanted or appreciated, or through friends. The result of such a change is that they will become less concerned with pleasing their spouse and more interested in satisfying their own priorities. The spouse will notice the change and become alarmed at the loss of caring concern. Their anxiety will rise at the meaning of this change, which they will interpret as a loss of interest in them, and they will put pressure on their spouse to revert to their previous habits. This will not happen, and quarrels and arguments will follow.

The shift from insecurity to security is often accompanied by a growth of self-esteem. The same applies to the development of independence from dependence. This self-esteem yearns for recognition and appreciation. The emerging person wants to cease being the one who gives adulation, to wanting to receive it. There is a whole reversal of emotional exchange and this utterly confuses the couple. All they know is that they are no longer behaving in the customary way. The developing

119

person challenges their partner, defies them, and refuses to placate them. They take on a new strength of character.

The same applies when the insecurity stems from fear of authority. Gradually figures of authority are no longer alarming or frightening, and so the frightened spouse stands up and challenges them. The challenge may be the refusal to cook, garden, fit in with prearranged commitments, answer back, or do what they are told. All this often applies to the wife, but equally it may fit in with a long-suffering husband.

Changes from insecurity to security may cause an upheaval in a marriage as the spouses change in their behaviour without realising what is happening. The change needs explaining to make sense of it.

Lack of awareness of spouse's problem

The whole of this book has been written with the experience of thirty years of counselling and seeing couples in action. When a couple are in the midst of a changing relationship they are not aware or clear what is happening to them. They will come to the counsellor with a story of escalating arguments, the certainty that one or the other, or both, are changing, or there is a growing indifference. It is the arguments or the indifference which is couched in moral language that hits the consciousness of partners. They are told by their spouse that they are selfish, lazy, self-centred, egoistical, proud, drunk with success, intolerant, uncaring, because they do not understand the problem and the change that is taking place in their partner. It takes a lot of insight to appreciate that a partner is changing and needs something different from you. The same applies to oneself. It takes a lot of time to recognise that one is changing from dependence to independence, from insecurity to security, from self-rejection to self-acceptance, which makes one less frightened, guilty, compliant, placating. In particular, if one does not recognise these changes as valid, one may be influenced by the criteria of one's partner, and feel that one is rotten for wanting these changes or failing to recognise the legitimacy of one's particular changes. All this

120

has been captured neatly in the phrase that the 'worm has turned', or that one is no longer a 'doormat'.

The trouble is that one has been angry for so long that when the time comes for change one is so furious with one's spouse that all that is desired is to get away. We take a long time to appreciate what is happening to us and our partner, and that an issue vital to our personality is at stake. In the end we are furious that our spouse did not detect our need much earlier on and respond to us when we were ready to receive their efforts.

The most common example is the wife who is living with a man who is demanding sexually and socially, wants a lot of sex, coupled with his food and household needs. He gets angry at the slightest irritation and is jealous and possessive, refusing his wife any freedom at all. Then the wife gains her confidence and declines to fit in with his demands. All hell is let loose. He is verbally and physically abusive, but she stands her ground and refuses to yield. Her time has come. She turns down sex, she may not cook for him, she goes out to her friends, and begins to put the husband second in her priorities. Suddenly the husband realises that he is on a losing wicket and begins to be conciliatory. At this point he expects his wife to praise him for his conversion, re-admit him to her bedroom, and return to her previous sweet state, but she does not. She is furious with her husband, and cannot easily be reconciled to his changed approach. He becomes dejected and despairing, and turns back to his old habits of coercion to try to get the concessions he wants.

This is a standard picture in counselling situations, brought about by changes in one spouse, usually the wife. Either partner may have been anxious, frightened, or feel guilty at the beginning of the relationship, and act out these emotions. It takes years for them to gain their independence, sensitivity, self-esteem, to recognise that they are behaving as the under-dog, and to their disadvantage. When they assert themselves, they have to work through the onslaught of their spouse who makes them feel either bad or mad for their new approach. Finally they have to overcome the feelings of badness or madness, and turn to counselling, or much more often to their solicitor and the law, to get away from their partner and seek justice for themselves and their children. Very often they are so disgruntled in the process of this journey and so angry that they do not want anything to do with the spouse who has put them through such a trial. That is why so many do not come to counselling, or only do so to get a stamp of approval of termination of their relationship. After so many years of struggle they give up hope of their spouse ever changing, and they realise anyway they want a different partner. That is why what is advocated in this book is the examination of marriages at regular intervals so that changes may be recognised at an early stage, when counselling or intervention may still be effective.

SEXUAL

The second phase is the period when sexual problems emerge. The first phase is one imbued with hope that the initial difficulties will be overcome, and they often are, but what persists remains in the foreground of this phase. These difficulties will appear in Chapter 16 and are only summarised here.

First of all, there may be lack of affection, preparation for intercourse and associated pleasure which persists. The husband is often not a good lover, and both affection and intimacy are difficult to negotiate. These couples may remain together and have sporadic sex which is carried out for the sake of relief from sexual tension. When the difficulty lies with the wife, she may occasionally find that a certain amount of drink relaxes her, giving her a gay abandonment and she enjoys sex, but usually the couple proceed year after year with a poor sex life. This may be interrupted by an affair.

A recurring pattern is one in which the man is brought along to counselling because he shows very little interest in sex. The physical and laboratory examination shows no abnormality, and the wife is seen, or the couple are seen together. What emerges is that the wife is aggressive and dominating, and puts her husband down at regular intervals.

He is compliant outwardly, but rages with anger and resentment inwardly. The result is that he does not approach his wife for weeks or months at a time. The absence of sex and affection makes the wife even more belligerent, and a vicious circle is established of anger, frustration and poor sex. These patterns need to be recognised in order to interrupt them.

As far as the wife is concerned, she may be left with a functional disturbance of pain on intercourse, or absent or intermittent orgasm and consequent lack of desire for sex, which may be independent of either of these problems. The husband may have a poor sexual drive, associated with premature ejaculation, and intermittent episodes of impotence. Generally serious impotence is a development of the third phase. The couple may also face the problem of sexual variations (see Chapter 16).

The most common sexual difficulty in this phase is that the couple will be faced with an episode of infidelity, which has to be placed in the context of the category to which it belongs. Is it a one night stand of pure sexual attraction? Is it an expression of erotic and personal significance, without threatening the relationship, or is the affair an indication of a terminal rejection of the marriage? Very often the first variety is not communicated to the partner unless some venereal disease is caught, which of necessity involves the spouse. The second pattern is sooner or later found out, and is either brought to an end slowly or suddenly, or tolerated. The third variety has a way of terminating by the very nature of events.

In most instances of infidelity there is no reason for terminating the marriage (Chapter 17). There is a need for forgiveness, but even more important, to go beyond forgiveness, which is to go beyond anger at being displaced, the frustration of what the third party is providing, and the lack of trust to understand the contribution of the so-called innocent party. Beyond forgiveness means that there is a need to understand the conscious, and as far as possible unconscious, emotional and sexual requirements of the partner who has had the affair and try to meet them. This is in opposition to the old-fashioned view that the adulterer or adulteress is in the wrong, should show repentance and a firm commitment to mend their ways.

This is a morality based on self-control which has its own value but has been superseded by one in which we need to understand what motivates human beings and try to reach out to the depths of their being.

INTELLECTUAL

Changes during this phase usually involve the transformation of opinions, attitudes and values. The idealisation of youth may be replaced by the cynicism or reality of middle age. The reality of the first half of life may be softened by an awareness of the needs of our neighbour. Couples may become alienated from each other as one becomes more cynical, harsh, trusts people less and less, and feels that the only policy is that of self-preservation, clashing with the altruistic intentions of the partner. Political views may change, but they do not often offer food for conflict in a marriage. Spouses usually agree to differ on such issues. What matters is a change of attitude which involves altering the whole way of life. A spouse may decide to give up banking, medicine, legal work, and take up market gardening or acting. This means a whole upheaval of the family, not for business reasons but for aesthetic ones. Views may change on politics, morality, the meaning of life and its priorities. There may be clashes as the husband becomes more materialistic, and the wife wants to enjoy the quality of life, or the wife may become more ecological and the husband buys a car that burns even more petrol. These clashes of outlook are rarely severe enough to damage a marriage provided the social, emotional and sexual relationship is good.

SPIRITUAL

With the advent of large-scale ecumenism, the religious differences between couples are largely negotiated with goodwill and equanimity. There may be an occasional episode in which a spouse becomes overtly religious and spends a great deal

124

of time in church. Occasionally they join a movement which is intolerant of outsiders, and the spouse is placed on the fringe of the partner's priority, but these are rare situations.

Sometimes a husband may decide to become a priest in the Church of England and give up sometimes a lucrative appointment for the priesthood. In these circumstances the wife's willing consent is required.

Another source of conflict may be differing attitudes on the upbringing of children from the point of view of their religion. This may become a heated matter, but once again is rarely likely to lead to serious conflict.

One point needs mentioning, which is that during these two decades either spouse may stop going to church, may become agnostic or even atheistic. Such a change may be very distressing to the spouse, and a major upset in confidence, but it is not a serious source of marital conflict.

15

Marital Difficulties –
Third Phase

The third phase of marriage continues from the age of fifty to the death or departure of one spouse. This is a period that may last twenty to thirty years or even more. The extended third phase is a phenomenon of our century, and we do not know a great deal about it except that marital difficulties, separation and divorce continue into it. The majority of difficulties are a continuation of the ones seen in the second phase, but there are a number of specific issues which arise in this third phase.

SOCIAL

The main phenomenon of the third phase is the departure of the children. That is not to say that the children who leave do not continue to contact the parents, come to stay with them, use them for support, and, when they have their own children, use grandfather and grandmother as baby-minders. All this happens and brings about the integrating of the three generations. At its best this extended family milieu is one of the cohesive forces in society transmitting values, opinions and religion from one generation to the next. At a time when community is hard to find, this extended community is probably one of the most powerful integrating elements in western society.

All this is the positive side of the picture. There is a negative side as well. This happens when the children are alienated from their parents, do not meet or contact them. This is exceedingly painful for the parents who have devoted all those years to bringing them up. Sometimes the arrival of grandchildren may melt the ice, but even then blocks remain.

As far as the couples themselves are concerned, the departure of the children leaves them in a twosome state, returning to the dyad of their first phase before the children arrived. Normally they return to a relaxed, unencumbered state with more free time to enjoy each other's company and to take trips at home or abroad. This is a time to revitalise the intimacy that has been diluted in the second phase of marriage. Increasing good health allows the majority of couples to enter old age enjoying companionship, intimacy and, as we shall see, sex.

Once again this is the positive side. There are couples who, on losing sight of their children, wake up to find that they are meeting a stranger in each other. The wife has spent the last twenty years in the company of her children, and the husband with his work. They have lived their lives in parallel, she as the childbearer and rearer, and he as the provider. The dangers of the traditional teaching on marriage in which the raising and education of children was the primary end was simply that it emphasised children at the expense of the couple. This whole book recognises the importance of children, but unequivocally comes down on the side of spouses who are there before, during and after the children depart. The essence of marriage is built on the viability of the couple.

Previous generations, who emphasised children and the diminished status of women, should not be surprised that children become the sole solace of mothers, leaving husbands to get on with their work. That era is over in western society, but in large parts of the world the danger remains.

Returning to the estranged couple, they may find they have little in common with each other after the children have left, and they simply separate. They may or may not divorce. On close questioning, one finds that the emotional and sexual separation existed even before the children had left. The spouses were simply waiting for their departure to finalise a break that sometimes began right from the start of marriage. When the alienation is mutual, there is little pain in this

127

split, but, when one partner is still emotionally attached, there can be a great deal of distress. The attached spouse has to mourn the departure of their partner. If they hate being alone, their loneliness may lie heavily on them.

Some 20 per cent of marriages break up in this phase, and we have to learn a great deal more about the causes, but one point which I have mentioned already needs stressing, namely that a healthy emphasis on the couple means that when the children depart there is a residual resilience which holds them together in the absence of the unifying force of the offspring.

EMOTIONAL

One of the reasons why couples break up during this phase is that, even at this late stage, emotional transformations are taking place. The husband or wife is moving from dependence to independence, from insecurity to security, from lack of self-esteem to self-acceptance, with the consequence that they outgrow their partner.

Sometimes we find men and women in middle age who have failed to be rebellious, independent or enjoy themselves in their youth. Study, work or an early marriage kept them at their desk or at home with massive responsibilities. As these duties disappear, they have a fling during this period. They go abroad and have a one night stand. They get drunk. They have an extramarital relationship of a longer duration, knowing well enough that they will not leave their spouse. They build a new life as they emotionally realise characteristics of youth, initiative, sexual and erotic excitation and fun, which are associated with the exuberance of youth. They astonish their spouse, children and relatives by acting in what appears to be an irresponsible manner, but which for them is the capturing of the first spring of life. Within the Catholic Church a similar feature of late maturation can be seen in priests who leave the priesthood in their fifties and sixties and marry for the first time.

This late emotional development can bring a creative outburst of life, but can leave behind an amazed and thoroughly

128

unhappy partner, and astonished children who acquired a new 'mother' of similar age to themselves.

SEXUAL

The clearest biological manifestation of this phase is the advent of the menopause which occurs at about the age of fifty. Ovulation ceases, and so does the monthly period, and it heralds the end of procreation, but not that of sexual intercourse which goes on for twenty or thirty years beyond it. This is the clearest indication that any inevitable link between sex and reproduction is false. Apart from a limited biological contribution to a small sized family, the main purpose of sexual intercourse is the unity and love of the couple, and the fact that this feature was absent from the mainstream of theology for two thousand years of Christianity is a great defect in its thinking.

The menopause itself does not interfere with sexual intercourse which proceeds uninterrupted. A small percentage of women experience adverse symptoms at the menopause of sweating, flushes, insomnia, and offer these as excuses for avoiding sex. Studies show that in those instances where women experience sexual difficulties at the menopause, these existed beforehand, and are not specifically caused by it. When the symptoms are really unpleasant, replacement hormonal therapy can be used with advantage.

The main discovery of the last half a century is that sex is enjoyed and continues long after the menopause. The main problem against the continuation is male impotence. Studies from the time of Kinsey have shown that impotence, which is to date irreversible, rises during this phase in an accumulative manner and is the single most serious constraining factor.

During this period extramarital affairs continue. In the second phase of marriage both men and women can become anxious in their mid-life crisis, and seek extramarital relationships to reassure themselves that they are still attractive sexually. This need continues in the third phase, and affairs continue to occur. The reasons may be for purposes of reassurance, a continuation of a trend that started early in married life, a late flourishing of youthfulness, a late emotional development or an exploration of eroticism in a marriage that had become indifferent. Each instance has to be understood and explained to the spouse. Depending on what category it is, the marriage may or may not survive.

INTELLECTUAL

The principal feature of this third phase is the good health enjoyed physically and intellectually by the couple, but there may be a few people whose intellect deteriorates. The single most important aspect of cognitive damage is to the memory. Elderly people become forgetful, lose things, forget where they have put them, and in this way cause distress to their spouse.

Large-scale intellectual deterioration accompanies dementia, and one of the most distressing aspects of the third phase is the situation when one partner becomes gradually demented. Initially this is confined to loss of memory, poor recall of names, which causes acute distress to the individual. A great deal of love is required to go on caring for an intellectually deteriorating partner.

Another feature of old age is the development of paranoid attitudes. A certain number of elderly people become obsessed with their possessions which they believe are stolen, feel they are disliked, believe plots are arranged behind their backs for their destruction, feel threatened by poisoning, and they can put all this down to their spouse who, in the absence of a medical interpretation, feels very hurt. Occasionally the spouse no longer recognises their partner, and believes a stranger has invaded their bed or home. All this is the negative side of old age.

But the majority of couples traverse the sixties and seventies in good physical and mental health, and enjoy a happy old age together.

SPIRITUAL

As the years pass by and death looms ahead, a certain attitude about the next life has to be struck. Most people concentrate on the here and now, and do not bother about death. Others are preoccupied with it, and spiritual help may be needed. But the most powerful answer in marriage is a life lived in love, with the abiding conviction that God is love and a life based on love will continue in the next world.

16

Sexual Difficulties

GENERAL DIFFICULTIES

At the heart of sexual intercourse is the meeting between
the personal and the erotic. This is a statement that needs
clarifying. Mention has been made that childhood is the first
intimate relationship of personal love, and marriage is the
second one. That means that, if there are problems in the
personal dimension in the first intimate relationship, they will
appear in the second and may focus in the sexual act.

Thus, either partner may emerge with difficulties of intimacy through an avoidant attachment, that is, getting close
to another person may be difficult and the intimacy of sexual
intercourse highly threatening. Such a person finds closeness,
all forms of closeness, difficult, and so the sex act is particularly challenging.

Much more common is the emergence of a man or a woman
who feels emotionally deprived. They experience the feelings
of not being sufficiently loved, wanted or appreciated. This
can apply to either partner and when sex takes place they do
not enjoy it because they feel used and not loved. This is a
very common sexual problem, particularly for women who
often say, 'All you want is my body, not me.' Such a person
has real difficulty in feeling wanted for themselves. Initially
the sexual attraction they feel may give them a sense of
being loved and they respond to it with alacrity. Interestingly
enough, such people may approach sex with passionate desire
for it in the courtship period. When they marry they may
lose interest in sexual intercourse and become disenchanted
with it. Their partner is astonished. A few months ago they

were making passionate love; now their spouse is no longer interested and they fail to understand the transformation. The alternative behaviour is for the deprived individual to continue making love with a high frequency as a way of meeting their emotional needs. This applies to both sexes, but particularly the man who may find it difficult to reach his wife emotionally and uses sex as a substitute for affection. There are special difficulties when there is a combination of two emotionally deprived people in which the husband uses sex as an instrument of meeting his deprivation, and the wife, instead of feeling loved, considers herself used in the process. This is an incompatibility which is particularly devastating.

Psychologists take the view that sometimes the sex act is a way of exercising power over the partner. The husband or the wife who feels neglected, ignored, unimportant in the general sense of the word, feels that when it comes to sex they have a power in their hands which they can exercise over their partner. The wife, who feels ill-used or maltreated, may exert power over her husband in allowing or withholding sex. Independently of this hold over the partner, it is claimed that there is something particularly energising in sexual inter-course, and at the simplest level the macho man may feel that in being involved with sex he shows mastery over his wife who has given in to his powerful seductive powers. Feminist writers see the power struggle of the sexes culminating over coitus in which the man seduces and the woman submits. When a couple are relating to each other at the level of power, authority and submission, then clearly loving feelings may evaporate. Sex participates in the struggle for conquest and is no longer a freely loving donation of oneself. At the extreme end, such a power struggle becomes sado-masochistic in the widest sense of that word. The weak person, who is often designated as the wife, gives in to sex to please her husband, to keep him satisfied, to keep him quiet. Sex becomes a price to pay in order that the woman is looked after and provided for. In this sense when women are not emancipated they use the sex factor to buy attention, but this is no exchange of love, sex becomes a bargaining ploy. There can be little doubt that the free exchange of sexual love is an infinitely better basis for marital love than coerced sex, whatever the basis for coercion.

Another personal factor which intervenes in the readiness to have sexual intercourse is the presence of anger. Anger may be caused by any reason. Thus spouses can get angry because they feel their trust has been betrayed, their independence is not respected, they are not appreciated enough, are ignored, are not doing enough for the family, or some special request is ignored. They may be behaving irresponsibly or uncaringly. These are long-term issues. There may be short-term ones of rudeness, the angry retort, sarcasm, ridicule, humiliation which may upset the partner. When a spouse is angry the natural reaction is to retaliate or withdraw from intimacy, including sexual intercourse. One of the recurrent difficulties that couples experience is that one spouse is angry and the other seeks forgiveness or wants reconciliation, expecting immediate sex. Very often this happens, but sometimes the angry person cannot lose their hurt and pain immediately. They need time to get over their resentment. Their partner, who is impatient, does not appreciate this delay, and tension arises over the misunderstanding.

The above are psychological difficulties which alienate the couple at the personal level. There may be social ones as well. The social factors may affect either sex, but they usually weigh more heavily on the woman. There are three such social influences. The first is the attitude that sex is for children and, when the desired size of the family has been completed, there is no more need for sexual intercourse. This attitude was strongly reinforced by the Church's position, which at its worst gave the impression that all that marriage required was to have children, and the more the merrier. One would think that such a view has become obsolete, but there are still some societies which hold on tenaciously to this position and bring it with them when they move to western societies.

The second attitude is that sex is for men and that all women have to do is to please them. The relatively stronger physical sexual drive of men, their apparent need to have sex incessantly, their difficulty in being affectionate, all add to a picture that men want one thing, and are prepared to have it at any cost. It is women's emancipation that has made it increasingly clear that women also have sexual needs which are physical, but also require an affective component. Women need to feel loved as persons as well as sexually, whereas men are happy with short cuts to their physical needs.

The third social factor which has overtones of psychological elements is that sex is dirty. Here the attitude of the parents is particularly important. It can convey the feeling to the child that sex is dirty and guilt-ridden. In previous generations, when there were powerful taboos on sexuality and children were warned against masturbation, some people grew up with a powerful sense of discomfort over sexual matters. Sex, dirt and guilt were so intimately linked with each other that any expression of sex felt forbidden. Such links between sex, dirt and guilt may have been associated at home with a deadly hush on the topic, with no conversation on sexual matters. Nakedness may have been frowned upon, and the young person emerges from childhood with a combination of ignorance and distaste for the subject.

Of course it is possible that there may be physical problems with sexual arousal and the experience of sexual pleasure which are camouflaged by social explanation. Thus a spouse who does not enjoy sex for biological reasons, which are not understood, hides behind an acceptable social taboo.

Thus at the personal level it is possible that a couple may experience difficulties from psychological and social reasons which inhibit them from wanting or enjoying sex.

This personal side has to be united with the erotic one. The erotic dimension comprises desire, arousal, intercourse and the aftermath. It has been suggested several times already that men appear to have a more powerful sexual drive than women, which can be aroused at any time. We are learning that women also have sexual needs, and in individual circumstances these are as powerful as those of the man, although intensity fluctuates over the monthly sexual cycle. In most women sexual desire is linked with the mood.

When the atmosphere is cordial, affectionate and understanding and consideration has been shown, then a woman is more ready to respond erotically. The popular myth is the

135

picture of a dinner for two with candles and roses, giving a very private and emotional exchange. This may work, but the background relationship is important for a woman. Does she feel her husband is in touch with her, understands and/or appreciates her? This is the background against which sexual intercourse takes place. Men lapse into bad habits of neglecting this personal side, coming home late, eating their meal, watching TV or reading the newspaper, falling asleep, and then expecting to go upstairs and have sex. It is not surprising that their wife complains of headaches!

But, if the mood is right, there is still the phase of arousal. Here mutual excitation is desired. The man wants his genitals played with, and the wife her breasts, clitoris and vagina raised to a level of excitation. This foreplay is an important part of the sexual act. The man may simply ignore it and ask for penile intromission straight away, not be familiar with the wife's preferred arousal site, be too forceful and rough with his hands, or go through a cursory fumble and expect his wife to respond immediately. In the absence of the appropriate foreplay arousal, the wife may be totally uninvolved during sexual intercourse, praying that it will soon be over and, in the case of a couple of my patients, planning next week's menu and counting the cobwebs over the bed respectively. There are women who become excited at the slightest touch, and are aroused with the greatest ease, for whom foreplay is no problem, but the majority of women, and many men, need to be aroused so that they can enjoy sexual intercourse.

The act itself should last sufficiently long so that the couple enjoy a mutual orgasm, even if it is not simultaneous. We shall see below that some women fail ever to get an orgasm, and some may not get it every time. When the act has gone well, the pleasure of being in sexual contact with each other is satisfaction enough. As mentioned already, in some instances the husband may have to induce orgasm manually to relieve the sexual tension of his wife. A much rarer problem is the occasional situation when the husband has an orgasm but cannot ejaculate any sperm.

The aftermath of sexual intercourse is a highly pleasurable, enjoyable experience in the arms of each other, or in close contact. Some wives complain that after their husband has reached his climax he turns over and goes to sleep. If the wife has not had an orgasm, being left high and dry is not conducive to a loving aftermath. In any case, the period after the intense pleasure is one to be shared together, for the whole point of sexual intercourse is togetherness.

All these points can be corrected, and an effort be made to make sexual intercourse a genuine experience of mutual affection. The success of intercourse is obtained when the personal and the erotic are in tune and fuse with one another. Clearly they will not do so when there are the difficulties described above, but even in the absence of these problems sex may be carried out when the couple are tired, tense, irritable, or in some way distracted by outside events. They may be making love and be preoccupied with money, business worries, illness, the children, or some aspect of the future. In these circumstances sex will not be relaxed or satisfactory. Thus, not every act of sexual intercourse will be perfect. Some will be far from perfect, but at the very heart there will be an attempt at closeness.

A particularly distasteful aspect of sexual intercourse is one in which one spouse is drunk, or under the influence of drugs, and insists on having sex. This can be a degrading experience, for it is no act of love.

DETERIORATION IN RELATIONSHIP

The above difficulties often exist in the presence of a good and loving relationship. When the personal relationship begins seriously to deteriorate, then this is often reflected in less frequent, unsatisfactory, or absent sex. The complete cessation of sex is often a sinister symptom that something is seriously wrong.

The patterns of serious marital disturbance are worth noting again, in respect of a person who marries for the need of security and gradually discovers that they no longer need their partner to rescue them. The same applies to relationships which start on a basis of dependence and the spouse has outgrown their emotional dependence on their partner. The same applies to relationships where dominance and submission have existed, and the submissive person matures and no longer needs to be dominated by their spouse. There are other relationships in which the partner is not affectionate enough, is too aggressive or dismissive, is not remotely sensitive to one's needs. In these situations the deprived spouse does not feel loved enough. This is particularly the case when a spouse has a wounded childhood, growing up feeling unloved, and responds to the signals of a cold, unloving partner who is accepted on the basis that they continue the disturbance of childhood.

In all these situations the withdrawal from sex is accompanied by a feeling that they are no longer interested emotionally in their partner. Such men or women talk in the language of 'falling out of love' with their partner. In the terms used in this book, they have become detached emotionally from the spouse. Attachment is the means by which the relationship has been formed, and as long as the emotional attachment continues there is a bond which sustains the couple. When that goes, the person remains in the relationship out of habit, for the sake of the children, for religious reasons, because they cannot stand being alone or because they cannot cope with the stress of terminating the relationship. However, there is not a viable emotional relationship and sex ceases or becomes very infrequent.

Such sexual withdrawal in the absence of any residual emotional interest spells the death of the marriage. There is a shell in which the couples live, eat and sleep together, but the relationship is not viable. When this occurs, then the marriage is essentially over and the sexual difficulties are the symptom of a non-existent relationship.

BIOLOGICAL BASIS FOR LOSS OF SEXUAL INTEREST

There remains a biological basis for loss of sexual interest. The most common is a post-puerperal depression. A small number of women become depressed after the birth of their child. The depression may be shortlived for a few days, or a few weeks, or it may be more severe and last months. During this time the woman often loses her sexual feelings and has no desire for intercourse.

Depression is common in women, and may strike at other times than after the birth of a child. When a woman is depressed, she may lose her desire for sexual intercourse. This loss is also expressed by the man when he is depressed.

Sexual desire is closely connected with the hormone testosterone, and when this is missing for any reason sexual desire may be lost.

Prolonged pain from any source may be sexually incapacitating, and both men and women who are affected by rheumatoid conditions may find sex difficult to perform.

SEXUAL ABUSE

In the past decade a great deal of attention has been given to sexual abuse in children, which has been found to be significantly prevalent. It is quite clear that such an experience in childhood can leave its scars on the adult. Most of what we know of sexual abuse is that perpetrated on young girls, but boys can suffer as well. Young girls can be abused by their fathers, stepfathers and brothers. Little boys can suffer at the hands of their mother, siblings, and occasionally the father.

The person who has been abused approaches sex with the feeling of having been exploited rather than loved. They know the meaning of betrayal, and their trust in people is low. They have suffered pain, embarrassment, distress, humiliation sexually, and the adult experience is a mixture of hope and anticipated dread. They hope that this time they will be loved, desired, and not used as an object of abuse. If their partner is conscious of their hurt and their approach is sensitive and delicate, then healing can take place. If on the other hand the abused person receives a sexual approach of indifference, then their anticipated dread is confirmed.

SEXUAL DYSFUNCTIONS

Under sexual dysfunction will be described the common sexual difficulties which arise out of physical disturbance related to sexual intercourse in the presence of an intact and satisfactory marital relationship. These problems have attracted a great deal of medical attention in the past twenty-five years. Several textbooks deal in great detail with these difficulties. Only the briefest mention will be made here.

Non-consummation affects about 1 per cent of couples. In this instance the woman finds it very difficult or impossible to allow penetration which is felt to be very painful. The husband tries to penetrate, and at that moment the orifice of the vagina, indeed the whole vagina, goes into spasm and the penis meets a wall of resistance. Pushing against this resistance is extremely painful, and is naturally resisted. The husband retreats and tries again, but now the wife expects to be hurt and her resistance is doubled. This sets up a vicious circle, and the difficulty is reinforced, leading to non-consummation. Couples can present themselves to sexual clinics with the problem, or they can seek help in a fertility clinic when they fail to conceive. The remedy is usually simple. The wife is helped to learn how to relax her muscles, including the vagina. When this is achieved, the woman introduces dilators into her vagina which are there to help her to tolerate a penis-like object inside her without pain, and remain relaxed enough while she is doing it. Gradually she introduces dilators of larger size, and in due course, her finger. All the time she is gaining confidence that she can tolerate an object, and her husband may assist by introducing the dilators himself. Finally anxiety is overcome, and the couple can try active intercourse, usually with success.

In the male there are two common functional problems. One is impotence and the other is premature ejaculation. There are at least two forms of impotence, primary and secondary. Another description of it is erectile dysfunction, that is, the inability to have an erection or to maintain it after intromission. Primary impotence, which is rare, suggests that the man has never have an erection, while in secondary impo-

140

tence the man has been successful but fails on some occasions. There are many reasons for impotence, including physical and psychological causes. The most common is some form of apprehension in which the man becomes anxious by the occasion, the person with whom he is having sex, or the feelings that are aroused by the sexual occasion. The anxiety plays havoc with the nervous system that supplies the penis, and the blood engorgement which is responsible for the erection is not sustained. Secondary impotence is often amenable to help, and any sufferer is encouraged to seek help from a specialist in sexual dysfunctions.

The other common male sexual dysfunction is premature ejaculation. In this situation the man ejaculates too soon. Sometimes the orgasm with the ejaculation takes place even before intromission occurs, very often soon after the penis has entered the vagina.

The obvious problem is that the wife does not have a chance to be sexually excited before the husband ejaculates and brings intercourse to an end. Thus with impotence the cause is mainly related to an excessive excitation linked to an anxious make-up. Sometimes the answer to premature ejaculation is to wait for a short while and to have intercourse again soon afterwards. This second time the penis may remain erectile for a long period before the climax. Another form of traditional treatment is for the wife to place her thumb and forefinger at the tip of the penis and apply pressure. This stops the desire to ejaculate and after the feeling has subsided intercourse can restart, and the process of stop and restart may be helpful to premature ejaculation.

As far as the woman is concerned, two common problems are dyspareunia, which is the experience of pain during sexual intercourse, and anorgasmia, failure to have an orgasm. These two dysfunctions are associated with the specific fears that women have in relation to intercourse, and the same problem as men which is excessive anxiety and the inability to relax. The ability to relax is related to vaginal flaccidity and orgasmic response. Both these problems are complex and need specialised attention.

The treatment of sexual dysfunction depends basically on

discussion with the individual and the couple so that the specific symptom is related to past and current sexual trauma, and the general approach of Masters and Johnson which has become one of the cornerstones of sexual therapy. There is, of course, a range of physical treatments which try to reverse organic problems.

The talking therapy is the way that an individual or a couple can come in touch with their memories and feelings over sexual matters. Individuals may have been abused in their childhood, witnessed painful sexual scenes, or experienced sexual trauma in adult life. These painful moments may cause the person to anticipate a repeat of the distress, cause them to be anxious and want to avoid sex in any form. Talking about it brings the incident into focus and gradually empties it of the hurt and upset it is eliciting. Thus there is a mental strengthening which allows the person to face the frightening sex with a new resilience.

The above therapy is often combined with the Masters and Johnson approach which has been in operation for two decades. This is a way of desensitising the couple to the sexual fears by encouraging them to approach sexual intercourse step by step.

First of all, the couples are forbidden to have any sexual intercourse. This gives them relief from the pressure to perform sexually, which has become very distressing to them. The first step they are advised to take is to have a bath and then luxuriate in touching and rubbing each other with some aromatic lotion on the non-erotic parts of their bodies. The aim of this exercise is to give pleasure which is non-sexual, but it helps to relax them in close proximity to each other. In this way they become used to physical intimacy, and can be close to each other in a relaxed state. If they get aroused sexually, they are instructed to ignore this.

The next step is to proceed along the same lines and touch each other in the erotic parts of their body, the breasts, clitoris, vagina, the penis and any other part which is sexually exciting. The aim of this phase is to encourage the couple to be able to enjoy each other sexually in a relaxed state. Again they are forbidden to proceed to sexual intercourse.

142

The next step is to encourage the couple to take the first two steps for relaxed contact and erotic pleasuring, which then proceeds to penile intromission. The couple are allowed to enjoy being in sexual contact with penetration of the vagina, but they are told not to proceed to intercourse. They may, of course, reach orgasm.

Finally the couple are allowed to proceed to actual sexual intercourse, and by now they are often relaxed enough to enjoy it with no difficulty. The Masters and Johnson technique is used widely for a whole range of sexual dysfunctions.

SEXUAL VARIATIONS

The last issue which needs mentioning is that some individuals prefer to associate sexual arousal with certain non-sexual experiences. In the past these have been called deviations, but commentators have argued that in the majority of these desires there is nothing deviant about what is wished, and so there has been a shift of nomenclature and they are now called variations.

The most common sexual variation is the desire, usually of the man, to see his wife clothed in her underclothes, in a particular colour, which is often black. This is such a common wish that it hardly merits being considered unusual. This fetish, as it is called, moves on to desire the wife or the husband to dress in something smooth, like rubber. There is a whole industry providing men with rubber material. Sometimes the man wants to have intercourse on a rubber sheet. There is no object that cannot be treated as a fetish which is capable of arousing sexual excitement.

Some women find these desires of their husband acceptable, and there is no moral reason against them. Others object, with the feeling that they are being treated as objects and that it is the fetish which arouses their husband sexually and not the wife.

Another sexual variation takes the form of a wish to cross-dress during sexual intercourse. The husband wants to dress in female clothes, usually undergarments, and be involved

143

sexually in this way. Cross-dressing does not indicate homo-sexuality. These are separate conditions. The man who is aroused by cross-dressing is a common entity. These men often tell their girlfriends of their predilection, and women often co-operate with their desire and buy feminine clothing for them, but some find the desire unacceptable and will not co-operate.

The third common variation is sado-masochism. In this there is a desire of either sex to experience pain, humiliation or some form of restriction when the sensation desired is masochism, and to inflict it when the need is to be sadistic. Minor forms of sado-masochism are very common and, provided the form taken is acceptable to the couple, there is no harm done. Sado-masochism may take ugly forms and become unacceptable.

Some spouses are bisexual, that is, desire and have sexual intercourse with both men and women. This means that a spouse can have sex with their partner, and also someone of the same sex. Provided the spouse remains faithful to their wife, this tendency can be accepted.

All these variations may appear within a marriage, and spouses are variously surprised, astonished, and very uncomfortable, not knowing how to react. When anything beyond ordinary intercourse is asked, it can set off alarm bells. There is no reason why a couple cannot adapt to a sexual variation which is mutually acceptable. There is no moral objection provided the sexual integrity of the couple is retained.

But the most common sexual problem in marriage is infidelity, and this is the topic of the next chapter.

17

Infidelity

Infidelity is not a new problem. It goes back to biblical times and before, and we have the loving story in the Scriptures when our Lord forgives the woman taken in adultery. Infidelity continues today, and is considered by some to be on the increase, particularly by wives who are trying to catch up with their husband's traditional behaviour. There is no doubt that the widespread availability of contraception has made it easier as the fear of pregnancy has receded. It is variously calculated that up to 50 per cent of married men and women may indulge in an episode of infidelity. There is evidence that the more promiscuous the person was before marriage, the greater is the likelihood that he or she will have extramarital relationships after marriage.

TYPES

Although all sexual activity outside marriage is treated as infidelity, the nature of these acts varies, constituting different emotional and sexual meanings.

The first category is the one night stand. Widespread travelling by businessmen and women and academics and large-scale holidays abroad by millions of people have made the one night stand act of infidelity very common. It is a purely physical exchange in which two people who find each other attractive have sex. This act does not deserve the name of making love because there is no personal encounter. Such an encounter does not, of course, threaten the marriage, and there is no intention of leaving the matrimonial home. The main problem is that venereal disease, including AIDS, may be caught, and if no precautions are taken pregnancy may ensue, which is often complicated by abortion. The morality of such an act is clear in that sexual intercourse should involve a personal and sexual dimension, and in this case there is no personal dimension, and therefore it involves a clear violation of human integrity.

The next type is a transient infidelity which may last for months and sometimes years, in which there is no intention to break up the marriage but insistence on having the extra-marital relationship for the time being. These short-term infidelities are also very common, and they can occur with or without the spouse's knowledge. When the affair is discovered, the partner may insist that the liaison is brought to an end, or they may live with it.

The morality of these short-term infidelities concerns the fact that the spouse who is having the affair is devoting time, resources, feelings and commitments which belong to their partner. Furthermore the other party to the affair is being cheated of the full range of the relationship. They have to make do with what is left over from the marriage, and it is the married partner who has priority. The spouse is, of course, betrayed, and trust is eroded. In fact everyone is cheated.

The third group of infidelities is when the extramarital relationship is an indication of a serious threat to the marriage, which is considered over, and the affair is replacing it. This is the most serious variety because it often spells the end of the marriage. Frequently the individual is not clear whether the affair is of the second or third variety. This leads to confusion, uncertainty, heated arguments, and a lot of stress. The tension may last a long time as the uncertainty continues. The morality of this type of infidelity is the final betrayal of the spouse.

REASONS

If one asks the man or woman in the street why infidelity exists, they would say because of lust, that is, sexual attraction and its allurement. In other words, the popular view is that of hedonism. There is little doubt that sheer physical attraction plays an important role for the one night stand adultery, but that is not the whole story.

Emotional reasons often play a part. The spouse who seeks an extramarital affair of some duration is often seeking an avenue to experience parts of himself or herself which are not being realised within the marriage. One of the most common patterns is when the spouse feels that they are not contributing anything of value to their partner and someone comes along who makes them feel needed, appreciated and wanted. There is a recurrent pattern of a husband or wife relating to a spouse who is apparently self-sufficient and does not need anything from anybody. Another man or woman comes along who desires emotional attention, and makes the spouse feel that they are needed. This is the form of adultery that acts out a rescue fantasy. Another pattern is the spouse who is in need of emotional and sexual attention which they are not receiving. Unconsciously they are looking for what is defective in their life, and when they find someone they pounce.

Another twist to the story is that of the emotionally deprived spouse who never gets enough from their partner and is always looking for extra attention. Such men and women feel excessively deprived, and, whenever they feel recognised, wanted and appreciated by somebody else, there is the temptation to respond. The maltreated spouse who is seeking solace is an easy prey at the hands of somebody else. Alternatively, the spouse may not be fitting the image of their partner. A wife may be married to a husband who is not decisive, strong, dependable. She may long for someone to depend on, and she finds such a person. Another wife may be married to a husband who is insensitive and is not able to demonstrate feelings. She may long to be held, stroked and made love to in an affectionate way, and responds to such an overture. Yet another need is that of self-realisation. In these circumstances men and women want to assert themselves, and they rebel by having an affair. Commonly an affair is the result of boredom, and the seeking of some excitement, particularly the forbidden, secretive, furtive variety. Such an affair adds to the spice of life.

In all these respects men and women appear to gain something concrete from their experience. Some people maintain that affairs can keep marriages going, and defend them in this light. It is true that both sexes can discover new aspects of themselves in an affair. Commonly they find that their self-esteem rises in the course of the extramarital relationship, and they return to their partner much more assertive and affectionate. They may discover that they are sexually far more interesting than their partner made them feel. For some people affairs are short cuts to personal enhancement, and undoubtedly something has been gained by the experience. The gain is attained at a price of pain, cheating, betrayal, loss of trust and the difficulty in maintaining two relationships. Nevertheless the absolute condemnation of infidelity by Christianity fails to grasp that, although the experience is imperfect, infidelity can have positive aspects. This does not always happen. Disappointment, frustration, pain and betrayal can also be felt by everyone concerned. Ideally the positive experience which an affair may give should be striven for and gained within the marriage relationship. But neither society nor the Church has reached such a level of understanding of personal relationships to be able to offer the ideal, and so the incomplete and defective form continues.

RESPONSE

The traditional response to the adulterer has been condemnation with a sense of self-righteousness. This is very common and, of course, totally un-Christian. The genuine Christian response is forgiveness. The person who indicts simply pursues a line of keeping to the rules. This was precisely the position of the Pharisees which Jesus condemned. An attitude based on the law denies the whole Christian message which is that of love. So we need an approach of forgiveness, even though the relatives and friends are clamouring for blood. There is nothing more difficult than the position of the spouse who wants to forgive, but who is surrounded by a family who wants revenge and a divorce. They are saying, 'Don't trust him/her. They will do it again.'

But in the spirit of the message of this book, we must go beyond forgiveness. It is not enough to take back the erring partner, to be magnanimous and to humiliate by forgiveness. It is necessary to find out our contribution to the infidelity. On rare occasions there may be none, but often we are responsible partially for what happened. This interpretation goes against the neat and tidy attitude of those who want black and white situations to condemn and exalt. We have to ask ourselves whether we have been loving and understanding enough, whether we have done justice to the needs of our spouse, whether we have been emotionally and sexually available, and so on. This is hard work because the so-called innocent party is being asked to examine their conscience. This sounds unfair. I am sometimes told, when I take up this attitude, that I am condoning the act of infidelity and trying to find justification and extenuating circumstances for it. On the contrary, such an episode is an occasion to learn something about the marriage as a whole. It is a time of reflection, and we need to go beyond forgiveness, particularly if the spouse who has been unfaithful feels justified by their act.

Problems also arise when the person who is unfaithful cannot make up their mind whether to return or to leave the marriage. This is the person who often comes for counselling. One moment they are at home, and the next with their lover or mistress. This uncertainty may last for long periods, causing havoc and a lot of pain. The uncertainty may be due to the fact that the home is pulling because of children, obligation or a sense of guilt, but the heart and attraction remains outside the home. The wife or husband accepts their spouse back, only for them to leave again. Skilled counselling is needed to resolve this dilemma.

When the spouse returns home, there may be a clean break with the third party. This may be a condition for having the partner back. This clean break is sometimes achieved, but sometimes not. The actual relationship with the lover or mistress may have ceased, but feelings go on and there is an acute desire to know what is happening to the lover. This may lead to complications because letters and telephone calls are continued when formal promises have been made to cease contact. The lying is discovered by the spouse, and there is an almighty row.

Returning back is a delicate matter. The feeling which suffers most is trust. The wife of the husband who has had an affair cannot trust that the ten minutes' delay in returning from work is genuine – or has he been seeing her? Mistrust can haunt the spouse. This is particularly so when the partner has had problems with security and has anxious attachments. They have lived their whole life with the fear of being abandoned, and now they are facing the possibility directly. It is such men and women who are tormented by infidelity. Their fear becomes a real nightmare. Another element is competition. What has the third party got which the spouse has not?

Faithfulness is a basic need for couples. The whole basis of mutual trust depends on it. When the trust is breached, recapturing it takes time and the original position may never be regained. Faithfulness is a fundamental human need, and Christianity's insistence on it is a mere reflection of human integrity, but the pressures to infringe fidelity are great and every violation should be an occasion to examine the state of the relationship rather than taking up condemnatory positions. It is part of genuine loving, not only to forgive, but to go beyond forgiveness and try to understand the reasons for it which need repairing. Ideally all human needs should be met within the chosen relationship, but in practice this is not always possible. Again, ideally there should be constant examination of the ongoing relationship so that deficits can be repaired, but we have not reached the stage when routine assessments of marriages are the order of the day. Sometimes it requires an act of adultery to find out what is missing. When infidelity does take place, there is no reason for divorce. It should be seen as an occasion for deepening the relationship with mutual respect of the partners retained. Our Lord forgave the woman taken in adultery, but asked her to sin no more. Couples have to go beyond forgiveness and help each other to sin no more.

18

Parents versus Children

This chapter is not about how to be a good parent (there are
plenty of books about that subject) but about the much more
difficult challenge of how the parents can remain as a couple,
protecting their interests, meeting their own needs in the face
of those of their children. Traditionally the Roman Catholic
Church taught that the primary use of marriage is the procreation and education of children, and by implication the
couple had to subordinate their interests to those of the
children. Even without the background of such a teaching,
parents are laden with guilt when it comes to deciding
between their priorities and those of their children. What is
forgotten in all this is that the best interest of children is for
the parents to continue to devote time, affection and care to
each other so that they can generate the energy to look after
their children. Counsellors hear repeatedly the story of the
mother who was so preoccupied with the children that she
neglected the needs of her husband. This must be one of
the most familiar stories of marital difficulties. Equally the
husband who neglects to support his wife when the children
are growing up is a constant complaint on the lips of wives.
Neglected husbands have affairs, and marriages break up
unnecessarily. What follows is the briefest outline of what is
an extensive subject.

TRIANGULAR SITUATION

I begin the review of this topic with the familiar story that
Freud gave us, namely, that the parent/child relationship is

a triangular situation. Freud postulated that the little boy was attracted sexually to mother and wants to displace father from her affection. This is a desire that is cut short by the awareness that father is powerful, and the boy unconsciously fears castration. With this fear he gives up his desire for mother and identifies with the father. This is the famous Oedipus complex which we are all supposed to experience and to resolve by the age of five. The little girl has a more complicated journey from mother to father and back to mother which is the Electra complex. There are those who cannot accept the sexual basis of this complex, but would be hard pushed to deny that there is an emotional closeness between the little boy and mother which has to be transferred to father, and there is an attraction to father by the little girl which has to be transferred to mother. Basically there remains a triangular situation between children and their parents which is very strong, even if not always strictly sexual in nature.

This point is made at the start because there is an inherent splitting and sundering apart of parents by this tendency in children. Young children show preferred affection at times to one parent or another which is reciprocated and can be the cause of tension between parents if they are not aware of this possibility. The same applies to matters of discipline which can split parents wide apart. Children are notoriously capable of playing off one parent against the other by saying 'Mummy/Daddy said I can have this or that, or can do this or that'. Parents who are unsure of themselves and lack self-esteem can adjust their behaviour to curry favour with their children against the other parent. The rule is that parents must act together, be seen to act together, and appear to be fair.

TIME TOGETHER

When a baby arrives, there is a real danger that the parents will feel their child comes first at all times. Clearly as a baby it will need constant attention in feeding, changing and attending to its needs; but as it grows older, there is no doubt that time should be freed for the couple to go out together. This is where the Christian community should be available to provide baby-sitters. At first leaving the young baby feels like a crime. The mother is ringing at frequent intervals to find out how the baby is. The young mother may feel guilty about leaving the child in the care of somebody else. If the baby-sitter is the grandmother, there is a sense of confidence that the baby is in good hands. There is the constant feeling that no one can look after the child as well as the mother.

Time together is essential for the couple, and they should take one evening out per week, if possible, to remind themselves that they are husband and wife. This togetherness is one way of keeping close. There is also the danger that the new baby will become the centre of attention and to forget that the husband has needs and requires attention. It is all baby talk with the relatives and friends which is reported back to the husband. In this way the baby rules the household and, if care is not taken, the mother sinks into the baby world, and the father into his work. When he comes home, the conversation is centred on what the baby has done and achieved, and the husband's preoccupations go by the board.

The incessant preoccupation with the baby leaves the mother tired, and there is a danger that between housework and the baby she will neglect her appearance and may allow herself to put on weight.

The husband is in a double bind. He is conscious of the importance of the child and feels guilty about pushing his own needs forward. He acquiesces reluctantly and is resentful and frustrated underneath. He longs for a weekend away, and hesitantly puts forward the idea. His wife may think it is a good idea but be overwhelmed by the feeling of letting the child down and being fearful that any time away from it will be damaging. Modern psychological insights have left mothers with the feeling that being away from the child for any length of time amounts to neglect, which, of course, it does not if there are dependable substitutes.

The conflict may not be over the time the child is left, allowing the parents to take a short holiday together, but the mother's concern about leaving the crying baby on its own. If the baby frets easily, the parents are not allowed to spend any time together because the infant prevents it. It is important to learn that a certain amount of crying will do no harm to any baby that has been fed and is healthy. As the child gets older, the issue is about putting the older children to bed in good time for the parents to have some of the evening together. After all the ploys of one more goodnight story, a glass of water, going to the toilet, have been exhausted, parents should have time for themselves. The trouble is that by then one or both may be exhausted, and all they want is to go to bed and fall asleep. Nevertheless time should be made for each other.

Most mothers want to stay at home with their young children until they go to school. Some mothers find this impossible. They tear their hair out with the frustration of not working. They are torn between their need to work and their duty to their child. Clearly such a frustrated mother will tense up and convey this stress to their child. When the child is old enough, around two or three, and a capable baby-minder is found, work can be resumed without any worry. Some mothers choose to return to work immediately after the birth if there is a capable baby-minder.

But there is no doubt that parents are often laden with guilt feelings. Whenever their needs for time together conflict with the priority they feel they should give to their children, who are thought to be small, helpless and dependent, they are worried that if they put themselves first they will damage their child and that this damage will be permanent. They should rest assured that their children are far more resilient than they realise and should not feel guilty about taking time for themselves.

All the above considerations are multiplied when the child is handicapped in some way.

PARENTS' SEXUAL LIFE

I have described in Chapter 11 that parents need the sustaining power of sexual intercourse to give them the emotional strength to look after their children. The child drains the mother and she needs the constant reminder that she is an adult woman who has sexual meaning for her husband. So sexual intercourse is important while the children are growing up, but a series of obstacles which the children pose at various phases of their development have to be overcome.

As babies, they may exhaust the nurturing mother who becomes too tired for sex. Getting up at all hours of the night, coupled with breast feeding, may prove a very tiring combination. Sometimes this combination is reinforced by a post-puerperal depression which puts her off sex. Both the tiredness and the depression have to be recognised and, as far as the latter is concerned, attention should be given to treatment if the depression is persistent. For Roman Catholic couples, when the mother is breast feeding and ovulation may take time to return, and they are using the natural methods of birth regulation, special advice should be sought about having intercourse if another baby is not wanted immediately.

As the children grow older there should be a good understanding that the parents do have sexual intercourse, and the goodness and love bonding properties of this act should be freely communicated to the children.

QUARRELLING AND CHILDREN

There are parents who feel that any quarrel is bad form and should be avoided at all costs. In particular it should not take place before the children. This is not the case. Quarrelling, when it is not excessive, is a normal attribute of human behaviour. Children have feelings of anger, quarrel among themselves, and settle their differences. They should not be surprised to find that their parents have conflicts which need resolution. Quarrels are followed by forgiveness and reconciliation. All this has to be learned, and the parents are the source of learning.

But the quarrelling should not be a manifestation of naked aggression, physical violence or bouts of excessive alcohol consumption. Many children have memories of seeing or hearing their parents having violent arguments in which someone, usually the mother, was hurt. This is not good for the children.

Sometimes the husband or wife is hurtful physically or emotionally. They may be having an affair, or behaving badly in some other way. Should the distressed parents reveal the unacceptable behaviour of the other parent to the children? Children can only too easily be used as a way of attacking an errant spouse, but the good image of the parent should be protected as far as possible. At a certain stage towards the end of the first decade children know when there is something wrong, and they will ask questions. They should be told the truth, but without vengeance or the desire to blacken the image of the offending parent. At other times, particularly as the children become adolescent, they may make up their own mind and frankly tell one parent or another that they do not respect them. Everything should be done to preserve the image of both parents.

Children rely on both parents to learn values and the meaning of life. The parent should remain a source of trusted respect as long as possible. The other spouse should not use the children to pour out their bitterness. Sexually the children will identify with their own sex parent and get a glimpse of the opposite sex also through their parents. Girls should be growing up with a positive view of men through their fathers, and boys similarly have a good view of girls through their mother.

It is important that children should get an image of their parents as not being perfect but *good enough*. They should realise that their parents have limitations and imperfections, but above all that they love their children. A balanced view of imperfection where it exists with loving gives the children the feeling of being loved without idealising their parents. Children may learn from early on that parents love each other without necessarily approving all they do, and they too can love their parents with discretion about their actions.

DECISION MAKING

Parents naturally take decisions on behalf of their children when they are young, but it is never too early to consult them and give them choices. A three-year-old may be given the choice of what fruit it wants, and in this way learn from an early age to be a responsible person. Later on children should be consulted increasingly, and parents take notice of their decisions. It may come to pass that in such a democracy there may be tensions between what the children want and the desires of the parents. Parents should not systematically sacrifice themselves for their children, but should defer to them when they make a good case for what they want, giving them the feeling that the world is fair.

GENERAL

In general parents take a great deal of care to meet the needs of their children and to put them first in their consideration. This is how it should be. Children are dependent creatures, and need all the attention they can get, but parents are people in their own right and need to preserve their love and sexuality for each other. Young people have a way of dividing and ruling the household. They should not be allowed to do that. The balance between the requirements of the children and those of the parents is a fine one. The children are best served when the parents do not neglect their own needs.

19

Divorce

Some of the marital difficulties described in these chapters are negotiated, the rest lead to divorce. Divorce has escalated in the whole of western society since 1960. In fact in England and Wales the rise has been of the order of 600 per cent. In 1960 the number of divorces in England and Wales was about 25,000 annually. Currently they have risen to about 150,000. When nearly 150,000 children under sixteen are added, then some 450,000 people are involved annually. This is probably the single most important social upheaval in society and has widespread repercussions. At the present moment it is estimated that nearly 40 per cent of current marriages are heading for dissolution. In the USA the figure is 75 per cent. In fact the three countries leading the table in divorce are the USA, Russia and Britain, but all western societies have high divorce rates.

Why is there such an epidemic of divorce? No one has formulated a clear and precise explanation. What follows are personal observations based on research and interpretation of social changes. I offer three possible elucidations. The first is a global theory and is the most debatable, the second is based on social and psychological findings, and the third is highly personal and has already been described in the Chapters 13, 14, 15.

GLOBAL EXPLANATION

Divorce is not a new phenomenon. It was present at the time of Jesus, and permitted in Jewish law. The only debate was the grounds for it which varied between strict conditions to very easy ones. All that was changed by Jesus' teaching which argued in favour of permanence and interpreted Jewish permission as the hardness of man's heart. Jesus reverted to a strict indissolubility which has been preserved in all the western churches, although the Greek Orthodox, Roman Catholic and Protestant churches respond differently to actual breakdown. The Greek Orthodox permits second and third marriages on the basis of the economia of grace. The Roman Catholic Church has a very strict definition of indissolubility, namely that a properly consummated sacramental union cannot be dissolved, but has a long history of church tribunals which allow annulments. The Protestant churches vary between strict adherence to considerable flexibility. Nevertheless all these churches adhere to the teaching of Jesus that divorce is an undesirable event, basically inconsistent with the teaching of the New Testament.

As far as the civil law is concerned divorce passed into secular hands in England and Wales in 1857, and has been subject to a number of Divorce Acts, the latest major one being in 1969. Under the Divorce Reform Act 1969 (subsequently consolidated in the Matrimonial Causes Act 1973) the sole ground for divorce is the 'irretrievable breakdown of marriage'. Such a breakdown can be shown to exist in the presence of five facts:

(a) Adultery: that the Respondent has committed adultery and the Petitioner finds it intolerable to live with the Respondent

(b) Behaviour: that the Respondent has behaved in such a way that the Petitioner cannot reasonably be expected to live with the Respondent

(c) Desertion: that the Respondent has deserted the Petitioner for at least two years immediately before the presentation of the Petition

(d) Two years' separation: that the parties to the marriage have lived apart for a continuous period of at least two years immediately preceding the presentation of the

Petition and the Respondent consents to a Decree being granted

(e)   Five years' separation: that the parties to the marriage have lived apart for a continuous period of at least five years immediately preceding the presentation of the Petition.

In general the grounds of unacceptable behaviour predominate for woman petitioners, and adultery, followed by two years' separation, applies to men. At the time of writing, discussion is again in the forefront to change the divorce laws in favour of a straightforward irretrievable breakdown without grounds, which are said to poison the subsequent relationship of the couple and the children. These changes, taken in conjunction with those in other countries, have stressed the 'no fault' principle. Marriage is seen as a relationship, not a contract, and it either survives or it fails.

But what is the nature of the relationship and what forces motivate its survival or break-up? After this brief introduction I will proceed with the global explanation.

In the last 150 years there have been profound changes in the personal relationships of marriage. Brief references to these in Chapter 3 are repeated here because they are central to our understanding of divorce. In the early nineteenth century a couple had a life expectation of about forty or fifty years, and their togetherness was task-orientated. Most couples had to struggle to survive at work and at home. They were busy producing food, keeping warm and educating their children and keeping them healthy. There was no Health Service or state education, and social support was minimal. The energies of the couple were directed outwardly towards survival, keeping body and soul together, as they had been for thousands of years before. In the second half of the nineteenth century, education, and in the twentieth century, health care, were taken over by the state, relieving the couple of a great deal of responsibility, once again shifting the emphasis from external task-orientated togetherness to an energy-orientated interpersonality.

Despite these changes the couple were still saddled with

160

tasks. Traditionally the husband was looked upon as the provider, and the woman as the childbearer, rearer and housekeeper. These were instrumental tasks which survived for a long time, indeed right down to our own day, but little by little they are changing. The wife now works as well, and provision for the family is often a joint responsibility. Technology has helped to reduce working hours, and offers more leisure and time for togetherness. The progress of medicine has made pregnancy safe, with conception reliable and under the couple's control with contraception. The reduced family size that has ensued has freed women from a good deal of child-orientated tasks. Running the household has become easier, and has also freed women for more leisure. Men are slowly (only too slowly!) participating in household responsibilities. All this has changed further the togetherness from externally task-orientated factors to an interpersonal encounter of intimacy.

At the same time as these social changes are happening, two other major events have occurred. The first is the advent of Freud and dynamic psychology, with a new emphasis on sexuality, emotions, feelings and affection, particularly the latter. That is not to say that any of these features are new; they have always been present. What is new is the depth of understanding, their percolation into education, and the raising of children and interpersonal awareness. Thus the new emotional encounter of couples is impregnated with feelings and emotions which are now in the forefront of human expectations. Feelings and emotions are succinctly described under the term 'love'.

The second social factor is the emancipation of women, which has been proceeding for at least two centuries but has rapidly accelerated in the last thirty years. Women's emancipation means several things. Women are better at verbal ability, communication and dealing with feelings. All these have come to the fore in human relationships of intimacy. Women's expectations have risen in all these areas, and men are handicapped in a variety of ways. The egalitarian relationships required by the emancipation of women have thrown males off equilibrium. The new expectations in dem-

onstrating feelings and communication present special difficulties for men which may have genetic or social origins. A
good deal of research is needed in this area. The overall
result from women's emancipation is a basic new man-woman
relationship and a much lower tolerance by women of adverse
behaviour from men which would have been acceptable in
previous generations.

There are thus major changes in personal relationships
with a shift from task-orientated togetherness to an intimate
interpersonal encounter with the accent on sexuality and
affectivity, transmitted by affirmation and communication.
The fact is that these changes have all occurred with a rap-
idity that has given no time for proper assessment, evaluation
and effective educational and supportive measures to respond
to this changing situation. The gap between these changes
and an effective response in education and in society has been
filled by divorce. This has been made easier by two other
factors.

The first is that the basic Christian background of western
societies is particularly weak in its understanding and handling of the subjects of sex and women and, despite the fact
that 60 per cent to 70 per cent of first marriages still take
place in church, the churches have proved to be severely
impotent in grasping and responding to these changes.
Whereas the churches have a long tradition on education
and nursing, they have an appalling poverty of thought on
sexuality, which has been linked to procreation for two thousand years, now forming only a fraction of its dynamism.
Similarly, feelings have been supplanted in the West by
reason and the intellect. For these reasons the churches have
proved unable to grasp the essentials of change and respond
adequately to them. But Christianity has one momentous
weapon on its side; its belief that God is love and that human
love is a way of exploring divine love. In its recent thought,
the main Christian churches have identified the link between
marriage and love, and have eloquently described it. What is
needed is to put flesh on this insight, and this book is offered
with this aim clearly in mind.

So, if I am right at the global level, the advent of large-

162

scale divorce is due to a rapid transformation from task-orientated togetherness to a personal, emotional encounter which needs different education, social skills and support. In this respect the Christian community, with its parish-orientation, is one of the remaining visible entities to undertake the work of accurate response and could set the example for the rest of society. It will be argued that this should be one of its principal aims of evangelisation. Finally it must be recognised that divorce has become more socially acceptable.

SOCIAL AND PSYCHOLOGICAL FACTORS

Within the overall global transformation I have outlined above, sociologists and psychologists have identified certain characteristics which are related to divorce. The social factors are age, premarital pregnancy, early pregnancy, lack of assortative mating and social class.

As far as age is concerned, it has been shown repeatedly both in Britain and the USA that marriages under the age of twenty are more likely to break down. It may not be age itself, but the emotional and social immaturity associated with it that is responsible.

Premarital pregnancy and the arrival of a baby in the first few months of marriage have also been shown to be associated with high divorce rates. A pregnancy and the consequent child put constraints on the couple which may lead to resentment and frustration on the part of the wife. The combination of youthful marriage and premarital pregnancy has been shown to be a particularly adverse situation.

Sociologists have established with some certainty that in the seeking of a partner the field of eligibles is scanned and assortative mating takes place, that is, that like marries like. The similarity is in education, social background, age, financial position, race, religion, generally in social class. There is considerable evidence that, when this similarity is ignored, then the risk of divorce rises. There is a common-sense explanation in that the viability of the relationship needs a certain amount of similarity in all these areas. If barriers are crossed in these social factors, there is an added strain which may be the last straw.

When social class is considered, there is a clear inverse relationship between social class and divorce. The highest rates of divorce are to be found in the lowest socio-economic groups. It is the lowest socio-economic groups that are likely to combine youthful marriages, premarital pregnancy, immaturity, housing and economic difficulties.

The psychological factors associated with marital breakdown are less clear. Based on the social factors of assortative mating, it was postulated that this would apply to psychological factors and that stable people would marry stable partners, while neurotic ones would be matched by similar neurotic personalities, and that the latter would be more vulnerable. When this hypothesis was put to the test it was found that neurotic men did not marry neurotic women, but, when there was a further assessment a few years later, the women had become equally neurotic! Thus, we have an explanation, not of assortative mating, but of contaminating interaction. Nevertheless there are strong pointers that marital breakdown is associated markedly with personality disorder. This is not surprising in that both spouses have higher expectations, and this applies particularly to women so that the associated behaviour of aggression, alcoholism, gambling, drug-taking, infidelity, are no longer tolerated as they used to be, particularly when women were dependent on men for their survival.

Personality disorders, which play havoc with marriages, are notoriously confusing entities in psychology and psychiatry. The reason for this is that there are different theoretical frameworks for classification. The first is psychoanalytical, and depends on dynamic understanding of the growth of the personality. This is largely Freudian and post-Freudian, and has as its basis sexuality, aggression, feelings, emotions, affection and the capacity to form and sustain sexual and emotional relationships. This approach has been immensely productive and modern counselling has been largely derivative from dynamic psychology. The defect in this approach is that a great deal of divorce has been explained on psychological personality grounds, whereas it has been argued in this chapter that the epidemic of divorce is rooted in changing social factors which have to be addressed. Divorce is much more than psychological pathology, and the danger has been that widespread counselling has unwittingly given the impression that those who divorce are essentially disturbed personalities. Some of them certainly are, but we have failed to discern that what comes first is the surge of emotional intimacy arising from social factors, and only secondly the psychological mechanisms which explain partially, only partially, the actual problems. The failure to understand the social factors is a major defect of psychological thinking, and I, as a psychiatrist, readily admit that I have been as blind as my colleagues.

It can be stated with some certainty that whatever the origins of personality difficulties, the fact is that the personality plays a crucial role in the new dimensions of personal intimacy required by contemporary marriage, and so the only way forward is an interdisciplinary psycho-social approach which is the position taken in this book.

SPECIFIC FACTORS

Within the overall social global changes described, special social and psychological causes play a subsidiary role, and then finally divorce finds expression in the specific factors which are the author's own classification and have been described previously (chs 13, 14, 15).

CONSEQUENCES OF DIVORCE

When the committed Christian approaches such matters as divorce, adultery and promiscuity, he or she takes a stand by the teaching of Jesus perpetuated by the Church over the last two thousand years. No other measure is needed to claim that divorce is wrong. A great deal of respect is due to this position, but it is not sufficient. First of all, as a dutiful

Christian it is encumbent to understand in depth the words of Jesus. The Christian faith is based on the wonder of the Old and the New Testament, particularly the belief that Jesus fulfilled the covenant, and in his own teaching gave us the essentials to understand his Father. We need not only to obey, but to understand why Jesus taught what he did. In this way the mystery of God will be unfolded. Blind obedience, a favourite of many Christians of all denominations, is anathema to an authentic Christian life that rejoices, not in obedience, but in actually living the Kingdom of God. Jesus did not make obedience the supreme virtue, but love. In loving, he was actualising the will of his Father. We have to go beyond obedience to the actualisation of Jesus' teaching. Secondly, in a pluralistic society, Christian teaching cannot be taken for granted. We have to demonstrate that Christian teaching upholds human integrity and can be embraced by the non-Christian because it reflects authenticity. So we have to go beyond proclaiming the gospels.

We have to show that the gospel values are genuine human values which belong to everybody. So the questions we have to ask in all moral matters are the human consequences. What are the consequences of contraception, abortion, divorce, adultery, and so on? My book on sexual matters is entitled *Sexual Integrity: the answer to AIDS*. In our age and time the Christian truth can only be heard if its veracity is obvious, and that means that the teaching respects human integrity. The same applies to divorce. There are plenty of people who see marriage as a prison in which human distortion, not love, is mobilised. For them, and they littered the landscape in the 1960s, and 1970s, divorce is a liberating experience, the more the merrier. So we have to depart from Christian dogma and enter the world of social and psychological consequences. They have to speak in their own right. What follows is a summary of some of the main findings in Britain and the USA, divided between the impact on the adult and on the children.

166

Impact on spouses

Certain things cannot be easily measured. When two people enter a marriage they make the single biggest investment in their trust that they will love their spouse, and in return they will be loved back. When this effort fails, there is an inevitable serious knock to their hopes, expectations, trust and belief in human love. That so many enter into subsequent relationships is a triumph of hope over reality, but there is no denying that every divorce is a nail in the coffin of human love. A divorce is a betrayal of some of the deepest aspirations of the human spirit.

In practice few divorces take place suddenly. They are preceded by years of conflict and tension, with the consequent symptoms of anxiety, headaches, poor sleep, irritability, depression, tiredness and lack of energy. It has been estimated that these marital and family reasons are the most common ones for women to consult their doctor, and for men they come second after work.

As the tension escalates, the episodes of aggression, drinking bouts, depression, become more common, and the whole family is upset, including the children. There are experts who believe that such a global conflict is so damaging that divorce is the best solution. It is true that escalating aggression is damaging, but that is not to say that divorce is a better answer. In fact when the children themselves are questioned they are unequivocal that they want their parents to stay together and resolve their difficulties.

At the time of the separation, there is frequently a host of physical and psychological symptoms which are very suggestive of depression. In the immediate post-separation period, the tension and depression are manifested by weeping, increased smoking, drinking, poor sleep and appetite. Throughout the escalation of marital conflict and in the post-separation phase, there is an increase in parasuicide or attempted suicide. There is a grieving period after the loss of the spouse which usually persists for some months, but occasionally over years. For some the divorce combines a sadness with an accompanying relief that the stress is over, but many husbands and wives regret divorcing.

After the immediate period of the divorce, what happens to the adults depends on whether they form a subsequent relationship or remain single. There is very strong evidence that those who remain unattached are prey to increased psychological illness with much higher referrals to outpatient departments and of admission to psychiatric units. Studies from several countries have shown that the rate of suicide for the unattached divorcee is many times higher than for the general population. This increased tendency to disease applies to physical conditions such as cancer, heart disease and accidents. Thus the divorced individual who remains unattached is an infinitely more vulnerable being, physically and psychologically.

A very high percentage of divorced people remarry. Official figures lately show that remarriage is not so popular, and it has been replaced by cohabitation. We shall have to wait to see whether the cohabitation phase continues to marriage. There is common agreement that these second marriages are more likely to break down. In theory second marriages ought to be more resilient since the couple should have learned from the first experience. In fact second marriages present problems because the same intractable characteristics in the personality persist, the lessons from the first marriage have not been learned, and the presence of stepchildren adds a great deal of tension. A percentage of subsequent marriages do well, but what we are all learning is that no contemporary marriage is free from the challenge of interpersonal intimacy, and sustained effort is needed in all marriages.

Impact on children

In a certain sense, adults are able to look after themselves, even though their experiences are acutely painful. The impact on children is a different matter. Children are dependent on their parents, and the atmosphere they create for them. It is beyond dispute that a child prefers to have both parents rather than only one. A good deal of the research of the last

168

decade has shown that children do not want their parents to split up, but does divorce have adverse impact on children? The evidence that is accumulating shows unequivocally that many, but not all, children suffer as a consequence of divorce. I will take the findings for Britain and the USA separately.

In Britain, as in the USA, there are a number of isolated papers from clinicians who comment on examples they see in their clinics. These are often loaded with children who come from divorced and separated homes, but they are unsatisfactory samples because they do not have matched controls. Much better evidence about the impact of divorce on children comes from three longitudinal studies in which divorced families can be compared with intact ones. The first one began in 1946. A sample of children born on 3–9 March comprising all single, legitimate births to wives of non-manual and agricultural workers, gave a population of 5,362 children, which have been continuously followed up. The second study began in 1958, and is a national follow-up investigation comprising 17,000 children born during the week 3–9 March of that year. Contact has been maintained so far up to the age of twenty-three. The third study began in 1970, and it follows a national population of 13,000 children born between 5 and 11 April.

Most of the data comes from the 1946 cohorts, but information that is emerging from the other cohorts supports the 1946 findings. In the 1946 study it was shown that by the age of twenty-one a significantly higher percentage of boys convicted of an offence had experienced parental divorce or separation before they were aged five years, and this was particularly significant for those convicted of sexual and violent crimes.

In this study the boys in families broken by divorce or separated before the age of five showed bed-wetting which was persistent up to the age of fifteen. Health Visitors rated the mothers of these boys from divorced homes as less competent than other mothers, regardless of social class. Teachers significantly often rated parents from divorced families as less interested than others in their son's school progress, and boys from families broken in this way were significantly more often rated as poor or lazy workers at the age of eight years. Beyond

169

delinquency in the later teenage years and up to the age of twenty-six, there were significantly higher incidences of illegitimate births to women, own divorce or separation, admission to hospital for stomach ulcer, and adult colitis in men, and of emotional disturbances in men and women, and reduced chance of academic success in higher education.

Another paper using the same cohort study showed that children of divorced or separated parents were significantly more likely than other children to have no educational qualifications by the age of twenty-six years, and to have a significantly reduced chance of getting qualifications at any level. This association was maintained, regardless of the social class of the family at the time of the family break-up. By comparison, parental death (usually the father) seems to have had very little impact on the child's later educational achievement. Remarriage seems apparently to have had little impact on educational achievement. The authors make this pertinent remark in 1986:

> Although social work and other caring services have changed considerably since the time these children experienced parental break, and even though attitudes to divorce and separation have also changed, it nevertheless seems likely that the emotional disruption that inevitably occurs in parental divorce and separation will still today be a crucial part of this experience for children.

In the USA there have been both longitudinal studies of the cohort variety as in Britain, and individual ones with matched controls. The American studies are more psychodynamic, that is, stressing the impact on the personality of the emerging person.

The National Summary of Children carried out by Furstenberg began in 1976 with 2,274 children between the ages of seven and eleven. In 1981 a sample of 1,428 children were followed up. The study showed that those children who had experienced marital dissolution were significantly worse off than those who had not, with respect to several measures of problem behaviour, academic performance and psychological

170

distress, exactly as in Britain. The most startling finding in this study was that 23 per cent of the fathers had had no contact with their sons and daughters during the entire preceding year. The researchers conclude that 'marital disruption effectively destroys the ongoing relationship between children and the biological parent living outside the home in a majority of families'.

I would like to comment on two well-known individual studies, those of Wallerstein and Kelly, and Hetherington.

Wallerstein's study consisted of 131 children aged three to eighteen at the time of separation. The children were followed up to fifteen years. At five years, moderate to severe depression was present in over one-third of the entire original sample. By the ten-year mark a significant number still spoke sorrowfully of their emotional and economic deprivation, and wistfully of their earlier life within the intact family. Reconciliation fantasies were still discernible in half the sample. At ten years follow-up, the older group ranged from age nineteen to twenty-nine, and they looked back over the post-divorce years with predominant feelings of restrained sadness, remaining resentment of their parents, and a wistful sense of having missed out on growing up in an intact family. A significant number at this stage appeared to be troubled, drifting and under-achieving. At fifteen years, half of the children were worried, under-achieving, self-deprecating and sometimes very angry.

The Hetherington sample consisted of 144 well-educated middle-class parents and their children, half of whom were divorced and the other half non-divorced. Reports from the immediate aftermath of the legal divorce showed high emotional distress and serious behavioural problems among the children. At the six-year follow-up, by which time the children were ten years old, the data showed that mother-son relationships in the divorced families and the parent-son/parent-daughter relationships in the newly remarried families were all problematic. It is apparent in this study that a significant number of these children who experienced their parents' divorce at age four will enter their adolescence many years later under severe handicap.

Thus, both British and American studies show a remarkable agreement of widespread short-term behavioural disturbance, and long-term social, economic and psychological disadvantage, with the worst effect of all that these divorced children have a higher chance of ending up divorced themselves, thus instituting a vicious circle.

Single parents and their children

In 1986 it was calculated that there were one million one-parent families looking after 1.6 million children. Every piece of research shows that these one-parent families are seriously economically handicapped, and that the mother (it is usually the mother) is under stress, over-tired, harassed, and unable to give due time and attention to the children, work and personal life. Undoubtedly more relief could be given financially, but the strain is more than an economic one.

Public cost

I have shown above that there is a private agony, but there is also a large public cost to the country consisting of social benefits, legal costs, the expense of taking children into care, and additional costs to the National Health Service and industry. A conservative estimated cost is of the order of £1–2 billion a year, and it could be £3 billion.

CONCLUSION

This chapter has shown that there are powerful social forces producing historical changes in marriage, coupled with rising expectations, and the gap between these rapid changes and an effective response has been filled by divorce. The consequences of divorce are extremely serious, and it is doubtful whether society or the Church has appreciated how serious they are. In this country 40 per cent of current marriages are heading for divorce; in the USA it is estimated that the figure

172

is 75 per cent. The mind boggles at the implications of such a rate.

It seems to me that, as far as Christianity is concerned, the changes in marriage and marital breakdown have to become an urgent priority, eclipsing all other social issues. I have said this before. The reason why I am repeating it is the obvious one, that marriage and the family are the root of society and the Church, and when they are in distress everything else suffers in consequence. All we do is spend money and resources to look after disturbed children in schools and clinics, sick people in surgeries, delinquents in courts, build more abodes to house the divorced couple, spend billions to ward off economic distress and, above all, create a vicious circle in which the divorced children of today are the divorced parents of tomorrow. It is astonishing how little importance has been paid by Church leaders, with few exceptions, to this issue. The silence is incomprehensible. Such energy as has been spent is more concerned with picking up the pieces, which relates how to respond to the divorces. I am the last person to deny the pastoral needs of the separated and divorced, but the urgent matter is to have a research programme to understand why large-scale divorce is happening, and what we can do to prevent it. There is no reason for complacency, for the Christian community is not specifically protected from the ravages of marital breakdown. A programme of effective research is costly and demanding. The churches have to decide between the priority of education and the family. I have no doubt which should come first, but where is the concerted effort to put the family at the top?

The need for both initiatives by the churches and an ecumenical approach in this country in liaison with other western countries is desperately urgent.

20

Counselling

The response to marriage difficulties has been large-scale counselling. In Britain the process started before the Second World War with the National Marriage Guidance Council, now called RELATE, followed after the war by the Catholic Marriage Advisory Council, the Tavistock Institute of Marital Studies, and the Jewish Marriage Council. These four bodies receive a grant from the Home Office for their counselling, but the funds available are not meant to be used for research.

In 1971 the Marriage Research Centre was set up by the author at the Central Middlesex Hospital, London, to provide a basis of research for prevention of marital breakdown. The inspiration of setting up this centre, which was renamed ONE plus ONE in 1990, is undoubtedly my Christian background, but I wanted to open the services of the unit to the whole of society on a non-denominational basis. In 1990 the Home Office recognised the innovative approach of the centre, with its emphasis on research and prevention, and made it the first marriage body to be recognised formally for several decades. The grant of £15,000 is, of course, far short of the needs of ONE plus ONE, which is a registered charity and depends on the financial support of society for its continuation.

The marriage organisations are primarily concerned with marriage counselling. The Tavistock Institute of Marital Studies has been linked with the dynamic approach to the marital relationship, and has been very influential in the counselling that has spread in the community. While marriage counselling has proliferated as one of the main answers to marital difficulties, the majority of those who divorce do not use it, and study after study has shown that, when people have marital difficulties, they consult first their relatives and friends, and the most common professional they approach is their doctor. They often associate marriage counselling with a sense of failure, and generally women use it much more than men. At the end of this chapter a critique will be offered of marriage counselling, but I want now to consider what happens when marriage counselling is undertaken. No two counsellors work in exactly the same way, but some generalisations can be applied.

It is very much better to see a couple together, but sometimes the husband or wife are seen individually. The remarks that follow apply to the couple being seen together.

When the couple arrive they do not know what to expect. They fear condemnation, they often want the therapist to take their side, and convince the spouse of their erring ways. Above all they want a magical solution. It is important to establish rapport between the therapist and the couple, and to reassure them from the beginning that therapy is not a session of moral judgment, nor a matter of giving advice, although the therapist will be hard-pressed repeatedly for practical solutions to the problems faced.

In practice the therapist encourages the couple to tell their story, each in turn, while the other listens. Interruptions are discouraged, but clarifications are essential. Basically the thrust of counselling is to move from the existing paralysis and the tone of mutual judgmental criticism to establishing what the spouses need from each other which they are not getting, and why.

The essentials of counselling are to go beyond the anger and criticism to the mutual needs and to establish why these are not being met. Do spouses really appreciate what the other wants, and what is it that is preventing them from giving and receiving it? The therapist will interpret what the couple need, but if they do not know, an enquiry can be made on the differences at the social, emotional, sexual, intellectual and spiritual level. Basically, most marital problems surround the issues of sex, affection, availability and money, and of these affection and sex predominate.

In the course of counselling, counsellors will ensure that they do not take sides with either partner, favour the husband or the wife, or be seen to identify with the cause of either. Recognition, identification of problems and facilitation of answers is the counsellor's task. Traditionally it is the couple who find the answers, but the counsellor is there to make the task easier. How is this done? At present there are two basic forms of counselling, the dynamic and the behavioural, and these will be briefly described, not from the point of view of teaching the method, but for some appreciation of what is involved.

DYNAMIC COUNSELLING

Dynamic counselling is the most common form used the world over, and is a derivative of psychoanalytic and psychothera-peutic processes, although a whole variety of modifications have taken place.

At the heart of this approach is the basic psychodynamic belief that each individual establishes their personality on the basis of their family interaction with parents and siblings. The emphasis is on the feelings and emotions experienced in childhood, and primary attention is paid to anger, love and sex. In this model, genetic factors do not play a prominent part. What is stressed is the pattern of feelings laid down in the first decade of life which have been learned from the parents. If there have been traumatic, hurtful experiences, and in this model no one escapes these entirely, then defences are laid down and they influence the reaction of the indi-vidual. So men and women emerge from their adulthood with basic beliefs about how lovable, wanted, appreciated they are, with convictions about whether they can trust, rely on, expect affirmation from, or to be let down by other people. *Childhood is the first experience of emotional intimacy, and marriage becomes the second experience in which the spouse will be treated unconsciously with the same expectations.* This is the basic dynamic counselling model in which men and women marry one another on a basis of *conscious social* selection of age, background, education,

176

religion, race, *conscious psychological affinity* of what they like and dislike about each other and *unconscious* emotional collusion, in which the partner is chosen because they resemble or are dissimilar to one or both parents. When the unconscious characteristics are positive, the spouse is idealised and expected to be loving, affectionate, strong, reliable, generous, understanding, and so on, and the problems begin when they are not. When the unconscious characteristics are negative, the spouse is selected because they repeat the parental features of rejection, criticism, neglect, indifference and domination. In both instances difficulties arise, and dynamic counselling aims to resolve them.

It does this by rendering conscious what is unconscious, identifying the defences people use against each other, and moving on to a better understanding of reality by appreciating how their parents actually function and what they have realistically to offer.

There is no doubt that dynamically-based counselling has been immensely productive and rewarding, but it has its limitations. Couples do not easily accept the basis of the model, their unconscious motivation, the need for reality, the hard work that has to go into changing habits of a lifetime, abandoning cherished fantasies, seeing their spouse in a different light. Dynamic counselling may be able to explain the why of a situation, but underestimates the effort that is needed to change. Couples may need to be seen for months, sometimes for years. In the traditional dynamic counselling situation, two therapists are recommended, but this is, of course, highly impractical, expensive and is rarely followed.

Dynamic counselling is effective in the more intellectual, well-motivated couple, and can be most rewarding, but its non-directorial, non-interventionist approach has many problems as people expect to be directed, given advice, and they find this approach confusing and difficult to work with. The main theoretical objection with this approach is the belief that all marital problems stem from disturbed childhood experiences, which they do not. This whole approach has failed to appreciate that all marriages are under stress in modern society because of the shift from task-orientated

177

togetherness to an emotional, interpersonal encounter in which dynamic mechanisms play a part, but it is the social changes of intimacy that are the main reasons for the difficulties. The panacea to modern marriage is not more counselling at a late stage, but better education and support for contemporary marriage.

BEHAVIOURAL THERAPY

Some marital therapists became disenchanted with the dynamic model and moved on to an entirely different approach along the lines of behaviouristic psychology, which repudiates the dynamics of the situation and works on totally different principles.

Behavioural marital therapy depends on reciprocity negotiation and communication training.

In reciprocity negotiation there is a simple concept in which it is considered that effective marriages are much more mutually rewarding than troubled ones. In this approach the complaints of the couple are restated in wishes for a change in behaviour so as to eliminate the complaints. It is assumed here that there are no unconscious personality clashes, but the couple want more time, sex, empathy, affection, togetherness. In reciprocal negotiation, complaints becomes wishes, wishes become tasks, tasks are imposed reciprocally, and the carrying out of tasks is monitored by the one who requested them. Of course, for this approach to work what is needed is that the task must be reciprocal, accepted by both partners, be practicable, and apply to regularly repeated behaviour. This approach is simple, neat and effective when there are no underlying emotional and feeling difficulties which make it impossible to carry out the tasks.

The second element of behaviour therapy is communication training. A great deal of marital difficulty is due to the failure of couples to understand each other. Effective communication is a key to marital progress, and behaviour therapy has some valuable insights which are worth mentioning here.

Couples overgeneralise. For example, an angry husband

may say that his wife never does any housework when he means that something specific has been omitted. Spouses generalise and elicit the ire of their partner who simply denies the statement. 'So, I never clean the house. How do you think we have lived for the last ten years?'

Clinical observation and investigations have brought to our attention the presence of incongruence. A wife rages at her husband's failure to help at home, and the husband replies ironically, 'I agree completely with you, dear.'

Another example is vague references. The wife says 'All men are after one thing; they are all lechers.' The husband feels included in all mankind and begins to protest.

A common problem is impersonal statements. Here the wife or the husband does not ask their partner for a specific request but states, 'All men who are genuinely concerned about their home help their wife with the chores.' This means: 'You are not genuinely concerned about me.' This could be put directly, requesting help in the house.

Mention has been made of generalisation, but it is worth referring to it again. In the course of disputes spouses say to each other: 'He/she will never agree. He/she never does anything I want.' This generalisation needs to be translated into a specific complaint.

Yet another problem comes when the spouse reads one's mind, 'The only reason you are saying this is because you are angry about last night.' The wife resents the assumption that her husband knows what is going on inside her. This is an assault on her independence, a domination of her inner world, a presumption about her feelings and the denial of an initiative on her part, in which she is allowed to express freely what she feels. This assumption about the inner world of the spouse also takes place when one spouse says 'We both think X or Y'. In both instances the partner may take great delight in telling their spouse they are wrong.

Reciprocity negotiation and communication training are the main planks of behaviour therapy, but there are other more sophisticated techniques, designated as structural, using such concepts as boundaries between spouses, their personal territory, dependency, overprotection, enmeshment, symmetry, and complementarity which involve technicalities we need not bother ourselves with here.

A third approach is dependent on systems theory which is not used very commonly, but has underlying implications for all types of therapy.

CRITIQUE OF COUNSELLING

Counselling has been present for nearly fifty years, during which period divorce has escalated nearly 600 per cent and it is pertinent, therefore, to evaluate it.

In some cases counselling is very useful, but there is a widespread reality that couples do not use it as often as we would expect, and repeated studies show that, when in difficulties, they turn to relatives, friends and their doctor for help. For decades the agencies that provide counselling have received money from the Home Office for this work, and are reluctant to question the reason for their existence. In any case, they are right in saying that no obvious alternative exists to counselling.

The fact is that after being involved for over thirty years in counselling I have come to recognise some unpalatable facts. The statistics show that even RELATE, the biggest organisation, only sees 50,000 couples annually, when there are 150,000 divorces and possibly 150,000 couples who could benefit from it. Many couples do not use counselling. Men on the whole are reluctant to utilise its services; the majority of couples prefer to sort out their own problems, seeking help from relatives, friends and their doctor, and associate counselling with failure, personal and pathological. As far as the couples who are referred to me are concerned, some do very well, but many come too late, having exhausted all hope and motivation, and simply desire a certification of their incompatibility, a view shared by other therapists. In fact, RELATE only claims that they reconcile 15 per cent of the couples they see. All this is disappointing, but it does not mean that counselling must cease or that counsellors are not skilled people with a great deal to offer. It means that we have to think afresh how to use them in a way that is more rewarding.

I believe that we have to recognise that couples must remain motivated to persevere with their marriages. This is a social, religious, and ethical matter. The Christian churches have to reiterate the message about permanency, not as a negative command, but as the realisation of the wonderful gift of love. This means that a great deal more attention has to be paid to marriage as a source of fulfilment of human potential. Coupled with this positive attitude, we must come to appreciate the damage that marital breakdown inflicts on the children and the spouses, particularly the former. When this subject is mentioned, there is the fear that all we shall do is inculcate guilt in those who are divorced, or divorcing. The result has been that in some quarters divorce has been made to look reasonable, not damaging, and a very rational approach to modern reality. It is imperative that both society and the Church face realistically that marriage is in the throes of historic changes which need major challenge. The point is not to make anybody feel guilty, but to raise collective awareness and responsibilities.

I am suggesting that the way forward is to move from a programme of counselling at a late stage to prevention, intervening at much earlier stages when the couples still have hope and motivation to persevere with their relationship. This means that we have to work in our schools, youth clubs, in our churches, for preparation for marriage and support after the wedding, with an appropriate liturgy, and above all a leadership-inspired drive to put marriage on the map. Counsellors have already been used in the Catholic Marriage Advisory Council and RELATE, in schools, and in marriage preparation. This work needs to be reinforced and extended with current marriage counselling coming as a last resort.

We need to look at prevention as the major instrument of support for marriage, placing in the hands of the couple the means of pursuing their own destiny. The churches have to become communities of love which facilitate marriage. Part III opens with this topic.

Part III

Issues for the Christian Community

21

Support for Marriage

Throughout this book has run the suggestion that our future approach to marriage must recognise that there are historic changes occurring which are changing its nature and that the single protective approach of marriage counselling is not sufficient. We need to take a comprehensive look, switching our emphasis to prevention, and that means we must involve our schools, youth clubs, churches and industry, and the places of work. In this chapter I will outline what we can do within our Christian communities. I will confine my attention to material which is already available in this book.

SCHOOLS

It is during the school years that we have a chance to inculcate in children knowledge and values which are of permanent significance in their lives later on. There is no doubt that knowledge has been uppermost in the mind of educators, but values are equally important, and in the schools which are still influenced by Christian values the importance of loving personal relations cannot be exaggerated.

What can we offer to children? In the primary school we can give them an understanding of relating, with emphasis on authority, co-operation, fairness, justice, affection, pain, distress, forgiveness, reconciliation, and an elementary knowledge of biology. The school is a natural community not only of knowledge but of being. What is appropriate in a primary school is to instil in the child that the rudiment of elementary relationship is always love, and that means affection, conflict and its resolution, reconciliation have to be learned. Social psychologists have taught us the unfolding possibilities of children in personal relationships, and the school has to deepen what is latent in the nature of the child.

The secondary school often thinks that its main responsibility in moral education is to answer questions about contraception, abortion and sex. This is far from the truth. What we need to teach children, by which I mean make overt what is latent, is the natural history of biological development, the world of feelings and emotions, the difference between the sexes, an historical approach to marriage, and a contemporary appreciation of love and sex within which problems can be discussed.

It is my belief that an elementary study of marriage with its current issues should be part and parcel of every senior classroom. The education departments of the marriage organisations should have in hand the appropriate material and make it available to schools. But the main point is that no young man or woman should leave school without a basic outline of the differences of men and women, the world of feelings and the nature of marriage.

This education should continue in all youth clubs, especially those associated with the churches. Both at school and in the youth clubs marriage counsellors can be used either to do the teaching itself or to help the teachers with the education.

MARRIAGE PREPARATION

In the field of marriage preparation the Catholic Church has taken a commendable lead, but even here there is much confusion of what should be done. Should the pastor see the couple individually, together, and how often? Is the pastor the right person to do this work? Should couples be seen individually or in groups? There are no perfect answers because no research has been done in this country.

There are certain things, however, which can be said. Couples who want a church wedding should be encouraged to attend. Totally opposed as I am to any coercion in life, nevertheless I would submit that marriage preparation should be compulsory. The churches do not admit priests to their ranks without years of training. The state does not permit anyone to drive without passing a test. The professions demand arduous training. Marriage requires no less. I would say that a six to eight week course should be mandatory, taking place once or twice a year, in which all the couples preparing to get married in the following year are gathered together, given a talk followed by discussion, and/or pencil-paper strategies. The evening should last two hours, with a break halfway through, and the priest should get together a team of lay people who undertake the teaching. Below is a possible programme, based on material available in this book.

Session I   This is an introduction in which the couples meet each other, are helped to see that the course is not Bible-bashing but informative about human relationship. The main talk is based on the subject of selection of one's spouse. This should cover the social readiness for marriage in the decade between sixteen and twenty-five, that is, men and women leave home, are alone and long for coupling, want to establish a home of their own and acquire the status of being an adult within marriage.

Within this social framework there is a psychological emphasis on love based on social selection, in turn based on assortative mating and the mystery of falling in love.

A word should be said about the danger signals in the future relationship and how to face them. This session is based on Chapter 20 in this book.

Occasionally a couple may decide that they are not ready for marriage and withdraw or postpone their marriage, which will be a good thing.

Section II   *What do we mean by love?*

This session should cover three subjects. The first is the experience of love we have gained from our

187

childhood. The second is falling in love. The third is loving. These topics are based on Chapters 5, 7, 8, 9, 10.

Session III   Sexuality
This session covers the meaning of sex as a combination of the personal and the erotic. The value of sexual intercourse in sustaining, healing and growth, and its own intrinsic meaning. The place of children. Biology and children. But even more important, sexual intercourse should be seen as a uniting force. Birth regulation. These topics are based on Chapters 9, 10, 11.

Session IV   Marital difficulties
This session should concentrate on marital difficulties in Phase I and II of marriage, coupled with an outline on counselling and its available facilities. This topic is based on Chapters 13, 14, 20. This session should stress the importance of regular self-examination and the use of a course at times of Baptism, First Communion and Confirmation of the child.

Session V   Theology
By now it will have become clear that marriage preparation is not Bible-bashing. It will have introduced the idea that Christian marriage is a *secular reality taken up in the Lord and made into a divine mystery*. Then an account can be given of marriage in the Old Testament and the New Testament. This topic is covered by Chapters 1, 2, 3.

Session VI   The wedding
This should deal with details of the actual wedding, a topic which is not covered in this book.

Session VII   *A liturgy for marriage to take place in the church*
The course should finish with a liturgical event in which the couple renew their engagement promises, coupled with an additional subject. An

188

example of a liturgy is given in this book based on the author's experience, but churches should be encouraged to produce their own.

In some areas, marriage preparation is being organised on a couple-to-couple basis, which means that a trained married couple undertake the preparation of an individual couple. This may be applicable when there are only a few marriages each year in small parishes.

SUPPORT FOR MARRIAGE

In the section on counselling, reference has been made that all too often couples do not come to counselling at all, leave it too late, and have exhausted hope and motivation by the time they come. The clear lesson is that we need to support couples at a much earlier stage, and help them to review and assess their marriage at regular intervals. Pastorally we have to move from seeing the wedding as the conclusion of the Church's involvement to being the beginning. We need to support couples throughout their married cycle. We do not know how to do this effectively at present. Below are some suggestions how we might tackle the challenge.

Practical help

Families need practical help when there are young children, for example to provide baby-sitting. Every parish should have a rota of baby-sitters to provide facilities for the couple to go out one evening a week. Young children need looking after when the parents are sick, in hospital, or for some reason absent. Toddlers and their mothers need facilities to come together, arrange for play and meeting, and this should be a high priority in a parish. At a later stage, when the children are older, suitable youth clubs should be available for older children.

Support for families

In addition to practical help, families need to come together and support each other. One way of supporting families is the encouragement of the formation of groups of three or four couples which assemble together once a month to pray and reflect on the development of their marriage. The formation of one or more groups in a parish of the newly married for group discussion of their experience forms an extended community of the parish.

In addition to the formation of groups, parishes should organise a day's conference on marriage and the family every year in which themes mentioned in this book, such as the nature of love, the change from falling in love to loving, changes in the personality, sexuality, parenting, are discussed, and the day finishes with a liturgical event. A day like this could also help the couple assess their ongoing relationship in terms of physical and emotional availability, demonstration of affection, communication, resolution of conflict, healing and growth.

Sacraments

Traditionally we think of baptism, First Communion, Confirmation as a time for the children. They have to be prepared for the spiritual meaning of these sacraments, with an emphasis on the Christian community. But it is also a time for the parents to assess their own marriage, their sense of loving intimacy, and their preparedness to face the needs of their children.

At the time of baptism, the couples can be helped to see how well they are retaining their togetherness, whether the father is supporting his wife in the face of the challenge of the new arrival, if the wife remembers that in this phase of transition she has not to forget her husband as she gets overwhelmed by the needs of the baby. Both of them have to consider seriously the size of their family in the light of their new responsibilities. The other factor to be planned is the time the couple will spend together in the face of the baby's

190

demands. If the wife stops working, consideration should be given to her potential loneliness, withdrawal from work and its impact on self-esteem, and her new role as mother.

At First Communion the couple have been in a marital relationship for nearly a decade. This is the time to review the relationship in terms of its strengths and weaknesses, the needs that are being met, or not met. The couple can look at their social, emotional, sexual, intellectual and spiritual requirements, and see how they are faring. In turn they can look at their parenting, in particular the balance between themselves as a couple and the needs of their children.

Finally at Confirmation the couple can look at their marriage some fifteen years on with its main changes, the satisfaction and dissatisfaction with them, the sense of boredom, if any, and once again look at the various dimensions of the relationship. As far as their children are concerned, the parents need to assess their preparedness to face their adolescence.

Schools

There is a further possibility of this review taking place and that is at school. Each school can help the parents look at their relationship *vis-à-vis* the emerging needs of the children.

By now it is clear that a parish has extensive responsibilities for family life. This cannot be done by the parish priest, although he has to be the animator of this outlook. He needs a group of informed lay people who form a marriage/family committee to organise these activities.

22

Liturgy

Part of the comprehensive service to Marriage and the Family is a programme for the local schools, preparation for marriage, support for it which is rounded off by a liturgy for marriage. Once a year the whole community gathers in the church to celebrate marriage in a service in which themes of marital life are interwoven with suitable liturgical texts and a commentary. The themes can be love, faithfulness, conflict, forgiveness, gender issues, parenting, and many others. The time to celebrate this liturgy is at the discretion of each parish, but good moments are at the end of the marriage preparation, in which the engaged couples come together with the rest of the parish, at the conclusion of the one-day conference, or at any other special time. Below is one example of liturgy formulated by the author and tried in his parish church.

This liturgical event took place in November 1987. The church was decorated as for a wedding. A cushion with two wedding rings was carried in the procession and placed near the Bible. Organ, choirs and folk groups were all involved, and we used as many speakers as possible. We stressed that this celebration was for everyone of all ages, as we are all involved in marriage, either our own or that of our parents, relatives or friends. The celebration was followed by a social gathering in the church hall.

ORDER OF SERVICE

Reading   1 John 4:7–8, 12, 16

Hymn   during which entry of celebrant and procession

of Book of Gospels and cushion with wedding rings

Words of Welcome

Reading   Genesis 1: 27; 2: 18–24

Commentary 1   Persons – Relationship – Love

My task today is to comment on the cycle of married life and integrate it with the Scriptures. If we start with the two readings we have just heard, we find two or three ideas which are fundamental to married life. The first idea is that men and women were created in the image of God. This aspect of human sexuality is to be understood in the mystery of God himself. The second thing which comes from these readings is that this mystery is to be found in loving relationships between man and woman. When we talk about men and women being created in the image of God, most of us come to a full stop because we do not have a great understanding of the mystery of God. God is a mystery, but we have two or three basic ideas which guide us. We have to understand the mystery of God through three key words: we know that there are three *persons* in the Trinity; we know that they are in *relationship* with one another and we know that the key to this relationship is *love*. All life in this world, but particularly married life, if it is going to reflect the image of God, must have something to do with *persons* in *relationship* with one another, *loving* one another.

I want to say something about love. When we talk about loving one another, we talk about experiences which we learned in our childhood. Our first experience of life was to be loved by our parents and then, through that learning of love, all our loving in life takes place. But what do we mean by learning to be loved as a child? All the parents here will know that from the moment a baby is born, it forms a relationship, an attachment, first to mother, and then to father, so the rudiment of love is bonding with each other. The baby bonds with its mother, and that bonding is done by recognising her face and body, by hearing her voice and recognising it, and by being touched and touching. If we think about human love, looking at people we love, hearing their voices and touching them are absolutely crucial to our experience of loving.

Going back to the young baby, within that bond of love in the course of the next fifteen years of life, it will learn many things which are about love. It will learn to be recognised, to be wanted, to be appreciated. It will recognise how to give and how to receive. It will recognise the feelings of hope, desire and satisfaction. It will recognise very quickly conflict, anger, forgiveness and reconciliation. It will recognise trust and being trusted. These are the things through which we learn to love one another; to trust, to feel acceptable, to feel wanted, to feel appreciated, to give, to receive, to negotiate our conflicts. All this is our first experience of love in child-hood and gradually, over the next fifteen to eighteen years, we as children gradually separate from our parents. We begin a separate life, we leave home, we learn to make a living at work or we continue our studies. This is the period of adolescence in our late teens and early twenties, when we finally separate from our parents, and we are at that stage yearning to form a second intimate relationship with another man or another woman. In our next reading we will hear the words which describe the readiness and the yearning in all adolescents to find somebody to complement them in their lives.

Reading   Prayer of the Adolescent – Michael Quoist

Hymn   Do not be afraid

Commentary 2   Falling in Love

We left the young man or woman in their teens yearning for another to complement them in their life. This yearning is experienced by all of us in our adolescence, filled with the desire for closeness with a man or a woman, and this desire is experienced as sexual attraction and as the emotional experience of tenderness and affection. In our Christian tradition, sexuality and sexual attraction have always been respected as a gift from God. We have not always done justice

194

to this gift and in western society this experience of falling in love has been trivialised, and cheapened. At its best, what happens to all of us is that those sensations of the baby in feeling loved by watching its mother, by hearing her and by being touched, are repeated in our sexual attractions.

We look around and we respond to human beauty, to human characteristics of love. I know that in the media the emphasis is on the body; now there is no doubt at all that the body plays a very important part in sexual attraction, but all of us know that there is more to falling in love than being attracted by another body. It is a complementarity of body, of minds and of feelings. It is a yearning which God has put in all of us and most of us respond to this by falling in love with somebody.

I know from my own upbringing in the church – and many of you may share this experience – that there has been at times a conspiracy of silence, a hush about God's presence in sexual attraction. Gradually we are overcoming this resistance and we are beginning to appreciate this wonderful gift of human sexual attraction; but just to reassure you and to remind you that sexual attraction is nothing new, we have chosen as our next reading a passage from the Songs of Songs which is part of the Hebrew Scriptures, of the word of God, showing that two thousand years ago human love in its physical dimension was exalted. This is really a confirmation that, in our yearnings for one another, we are doing no more than responding to what God has inserted inside us as the means of finding love.

Reading	Song of Songs 4:9–11; 5:10–16
Hymn	The love I have for you, O Lord
Gospel Reading	John 15: 9–12
Renewal of Commitment	(made by a couple representing all the married couples)

Before God, and in the presence of all here present, and on behalf of all who are married and here this evening, I renew my commitment to you, my lawful wedded wife/husband to have and to hold from this day forward, for better for worse, for richer for poorer, in sickness and in health, to love and to cherish till death us do part.

Commentary 3   Unfolding Relationship of Love

That moment of commitment is the beginning of the sacrament of marriage. It is a moment of enormous importance in the life of two people. From now on they are going to have an unfolding relationship of love which may span forty or fifty years of their life and, psychologically, a great change is going to happen in their lives; that is, they are going to change from falling in love, from the idealisation of falling in love where they experience each other as the most beautiful person in the world, where they experience each other as being totally perfect in their behaviour, when they experience each other without fault; a few weeks of married life will tell them a different story.

That different story is the beginning of changing from falling in love to loving. From now on there will be the challenge of forty to fifty years of *loving* one another. When we use the word 'love', we still have an image of romantic love, idealised love, sexual love; but in fact 99 per cent of loving is to do with the way we relate to one another and what I want to say next is a summary of the essence of loving in human relationships and particularly in marriage. I believe that at the heart of loving in marriage are three things; the three things I have called Sustaining, Healing and Growth.

Sustaining – A couple will need the external framework of a house, a job, money – that is the external sustaining of each other. The internal sustaining of each other is to repeat in their second intimate relationship all the experiences of love that they have learned as children, to trust, to respect and care, to give, to receive, to negotiate conflict, to forgive, to understand one another. Everyone knows what I mean by this sustaining love. Nowadays we say that at the heart of this sustaining love is a yearning that two people have to know each other, to know the depths of the other, just as the

Father knows the Son, and the Son knows the Father, and both know the Spirit. For that, married couples need effective communication, talking, sharing, and understanding one another.

Healing – In the depths of revealing ourselves to one another, we not only reveal our strengths but we reveal our weaknesses and our wounds. If you spend a few days with another human being, you will soon find out their limitations. Married couples spend forty or fifty years with one another and they know very well each other's wounds. Some people feel totally unlovable, totally unloved, totally lacking in self-esteem, totally lacking in lovable feelings. But all of us have some of these problems; all of us at times feel persecuted and the wonderful thing about an intimate loving relationship – but particularly marriage – is that two people, a man and a woman, can give to each other another chance to feel unconditionally loved. If I am short of love or feel unlovable, my partner appreciates me again and again and I learn a new experience. If my partner lacks confidence, I give her reassurance and she grows in confidence and so on and so on. At the heart of this sacrament there is an enormous amount of healing, and in fact the Second Vatican Council used the word 'healing' as part of the grace of the inner life of this sacrament.

Growth – Beyond sustaining and healing there is growth. If we spend forty or fifty years together, we do not remain the same; we grow, we change. How do we grow? How do we change? Physically we come to marriage with our adult stature well established; the only thing we do over time is put inches around our waist and grow grey! The second thing that happens concerns our intelligence. We come to marriage with our intelligence well established but over the years our spouse is the person who listens to us day in and day out, and through their comments, appreciation and loving criticism, we change our experience of ourselves and our thoughts from intelligence to wisdom. Finally we grow in our capacity to love one another. Now we do terrible things to one another as married people and as friends, when it comes to loving.

We think that the best way to love our partner is to present the longest possible list of what is wrong with them and then ask our partner or friend to change. This litany of criticism is not love. At our Lord's baptism and Transfiguration, the heavens opened and a voice was heard which affirmed him as the beloved Son of the Father. At the heart of loving is affirmation. We need to be affirmed day in and day out, to be appreciated, to feel we are loved. Finally we have to learn to deal with conflict. Instead of seeing conflict as a battle to be won, we need to hear the anguish of the hurt one and respond by changing our behaviour.

So in these three ideas, in sustaining, in healing, in growth, lies the heart of loving. St Paul wrote a section about love which uses totally different language, but which expresses the same ideas which I have just shared with you.

Reading   1 Corinthians 13:1–8

Commentary 4   Sexuality, Body Language of Love, Life Giving, Children

If we use the word love in the context of marriage, we cannot escape from talking about sexual love. Some of you may think that talking about sexual love inside a church is really out of place; but, as I have been saying to you today, sexual love is really at the heart of the man/woman relationship reflecting the image of God. It is probably the most precious gift that God has given to mankind to bring about the kingdom of love we are talking about. For the last three thousand years sexual intercourse has been linked to procreation. Nowadays the overwhelming majority of sexual activity is knowingly, deliberately and consciously not procreative and the question that we all have to ask is, what is the meaning of sexual intercourse if it is not primarily linked with procreation?

For me, sexual intercourse is a precious gift from God, a recurrent act of body language of love. When two people are making love, they are speaking to one another with their bodies. What are they saying to each other? They are saying to each other at least five things. They are saying to each other, you are the most important person in my life. I recognise you, I want you, I appreciate you. It is a recurrent affirmation of personhood. When they are making love, the man makes the woman feel most completely feminine, and the woman makes the man feel most completely masculine. They are confirming each other's sexual identity. Thirdly, we all know that in the course of the day we argue, we quarrel, we hurt one another, and very quickly often we forget and forgive. But sometimes the pain is much too deep and it requires an act of love to heal it and it can therefore be an act of reconciliation. Fourthly, when we make love, by its very nature we want to repeat that act; in that act lies the permanent hope that our spouse will want us and love us again. It is a continuous experience of hope of being loved. Finally, when we make love, it is an act of thanksgiving for our partner's being, for their presence in our life and for their being available to us in this shared joy. In other words, sexual intercourse gives *life* to two people whenever it is carried out and on a few occasions it gives rise to a *new* life.

The link between sexual intercourse and children is, of course, biological but lies principally in the fact that children need love and security and sexual intercourse gives the strength, the bonding and the love to the parents to sustain each other and their children and to give their children the love which they need. Loving our children completes the cycle of love. Loving our children as God loves us, we give them the first experience of being recognised, wanted and appreciated; we give them the experience of trust, of giving and receiving, of empathy, of forgiveness, of understanding. But if we are going to be really loving parents, our task is to help them to grow and ultimately to leave us, find their own partners and repeat the cycle. This idea of acting as catalysts of growth for our children is beautifully captured in the book of *The Prophet*.

Reading   From *The Prophet* – Kahlil Gibran on Children

Commentary 5   *The Domestic Church, Community of Love, Our Married Spirituality*

199

I conclude my commentary with a word about theology. We live in a church that tries to understand the life of each one of us in our relationship with God. Theology is talking about God and the whole of this liturgy is relating marriage and the family to God. All of us know – because we have been taught – that marriage is a sacrament. In the past we have tended to concentrate on the wedding day. It is perfectly true that at the wedding a commitment is given and the sacrament begins, but that is not the end of the story.

The Second Vatican Council called Marriage and the Family a community of love, and our understanding of this sacrament nowadays is that a relationship of love unfolds over forty to fifty years of life of a husband and wife. In the Second Vatican Council it is called a covenant; marriage becomes the symbol of the promise by God to man.

It is called a relationship, and our understanding of this sacrament is really that it is a moment-to-moment encounter of loving. In that moment-to-moment encounter of loving, the ordinary becomes extraordinary, and so, in the course of the twenty-four hours of the day, as we get up, wash, dress, cook breakfast, go to work, take our children to school, as we come back and have our meal, as we talk to one another, as we make love, the moment-to-moment relating is the encounter of God in each other, of Christ in each other through this sacrament.

You are aware of the life of the priest: he has a special life. He says mass, he preaches, administers the sacrament and reads his breviary. You are aware of monastic life; you may have been in a monastery and have seen monks praying around the clock. The Catholic Church teaches us at the Second Vatican Council that all married people have a 'Domestic Church'. In the course of our daily life we have our own spirituality as we struggle to relate lovingly to one another; as we struggle to understand one another; as we make umpteen mistakes and we create umpteen hurts; as we reach one another umpteen times in the twenty-four hours; at those moments we encounter Christ in one another. This is the new theology, the theology of understanding marriage which we

200

live out in our own homes, and it is that experience that we bring to our Sunday Liturgy, that we bring to a liturgy like this, that is our spirituality, and one day the saints of the Church will be those who have struggled to sustain, to heal and to grow in each other.

Relating to one another and our children, that is our spirituality, that is our domestic church, and it is a church that belongs to all of us, whether we are single, married, separated, divorced or widowed; all of us have a domestic experience. Finally, this is not a domestic experience of a selfish mutuality, just two people engrossed with one another. In that little community of love, the more we love one another the more we open ourselves to our neighbours, to anybody around us in our parish, in our community.

The whole becomes a marriage feast in which we invite – as the gospel reminds us – everybody into our lives. It becomes the open space of loving. That is the domestic church; that is our spirituality, and it is that which we have come here to celebrate.

Silent Reflection

Prayer

Dear God, look with love upon us all here this evening. We ask your blessing; give us the grace of love and peace. May we always follow the example of the holy people whose praises are sung in the Scriptures. May we put our trust in each other and recognise that we are holy in your sight and heirs with each other to the life of grace. May we always honour and love each other as Christ loves his bride, the Church. Father, keep us always true to your commandments; keep those who are married faithful in marriage; be close to those who have lost their loved ones; be the partner of those whose vocation it is to be single; let us all be living and loving examples of Christian life; give us the strength which comes from the gospel; bless all our newlyweds with children, and help them to be good parents. Grant us all after a happy old age fullness of life with the saints in the kingdom of heaven.

We make our prayers in the name of Jesus who is Christ our
Lord. Amen.

Sign of Peace

Reading   1 John 4:7–8, 12–16

Hymn   Bind us together, Lord

Solemn Blessing

Father, by your power you have made everything out of
nothing. In the beginning you created the universe and made
mankind in your own likeness. You gave man the constant
help of woman so that man and woman should no longer be
two, but one flesh, and you teach that what you have united
may never be divided. You made the union of husband and
wife so holy a mystery that it symbolises the marriage of
Christ and his Church. Father, keep us always true to your
commandments. Keep us faithful in marriage, and may we
be living examples of Christian life.

May Almighty God bless you, in the name of the Father,
and of the Son, and of the Holy Spirit. Amen.

Hymn   O Lord, my God, when I in awesome wonder

23

Choosing a Partner

To avoid the pain of disillusionment and marital breakdown, young people need to choose wisely at the start of their relationship. Some of them, as we shall see, decide to live together beforehand, but the accumulative evidence suggests that cohabitation does not prevent breakdown of marriage. In this chapter evidence from research and the author's clinical acumen is put together as an outline of some of the points that need to be observed when choosing a partner. This approach recognises that falling in love is not always a conscious, deliberate choice, but the more that is known about the likely future, the better prepared are the couple to face each other. If it is known that an emotionally difficult partner has been chosen, then the spouse can face the ensuing difficulties with some equanimity and support.

SOCIAL FACTORS

The social factors have been mentioned already. Research evidence points out that marriages are built on social assortative mating, which means that like marries like. Thus, if a potential partner comes from a totally different age bracket, social class, education, economic standing, then extreme caution should be taken with such a union. After the emotional basis for the relationship settles down, the couple have to live on this social basis of their life. If this does not give them common ground, then difficulties may ensue.

Age at marriage has been shown repeatedly to reflect its outcome. Marriages before the age of twenty are extremely vulnerable. Evidence has also accumulated that premarital pregnancy or a baby in the early months of the marriage is associated with more marital vulnerability. In previous generations, when a man made a woman pregnant it was felt that duty required that marriage should ensue. We now realise that this is a wrong approach. Abortion is not the answer either. Many young women have babies and look after them without the father, or without the financial support of the father. Although single-parent families have their disadvantages, they are infinitely preferable to forced weddings when no love exists. Youthful marriages coupled with premarital pregnancies have the highest rate of marital breakdown and should be avoided at all cost. If these vulnerable relationships take place, the couple should be prepared for the difficulties ahead. These may be feelings of resentment for being tied down at such an early age, of missing out, being depressed after the birth of the baby, housing and financial difficulties, and a feeling of having been cheated of the fun of youth.

PSYCHOLOGICAL FACTORS

Personality factors

There is little doubt that marital breakdown is littered with couples in which one or both partners have problems in their personality. As already mentioned, psychologists have difficulty in defining personality problems. There are classifications based on the presence of a group of symptoms or dynamically-orientated problems. No differentiation will be made here, but a group of common difficulties will be briefly outlined.

Immature and psychopathic personality

This describes a man or woman who has a wide range of difficulties. They have a poor capacity to cope with frustration or delayed gratification. They want their instinctual pleasures immediately and cannot cope with any postponement of plea-sure. They are self-centred and largely think of themselves first. They have poor ability to cope with frustration and criticism. In the latter case they are very sensitive, and respond maximally to minimum hurts. Their work record is poor, and they move from jobs with flimsy excuses, whereas in practice they lack motivation, persistence, cannot cope with authority, and are unable to learn from experience. Sometimes they are intellectually and technically brilliant, but cannot work with others. When checked, disappointed or criticised, they respond with aggression which may be physi-cal or verbal. They may accompany all these symptoms with heavy drinking, gambling or drug-taking. In practice it is rare for all these symptoms to be present together, but such people betray themselves in several ways with their impatience, aggression, anger and inconsistency.

Paranoid personality

The paranoid person is apprehensive about others. The world is treated as potentially dangerous where everyone else is a hidden enemy who is going to attack. The world of the para-noid individual is sinister and not to be trusted. There is a good reason why people are bad and cannot be relied upon. Such men and women are sensitive to criticism, react violently to it, and sulk long afterwards. Like immature people, they find it very difficult to be in the wrong and to apologise. When something goes wrong, it is everybody else's fault but their own.

Dependent personality

The dependent personality has been mentioned already several times. It is one which relies on the other person for guidance, decision, initiative, and handling of difficulties. Such a person should avoid matching with an authoritarian, dominating figure who perpetuates their dependence. The intended spouse who recognises these dependent features in the partner should avoid colluding with them.

Deprived personality

The deprived individual has grown up hungry for affection. The reasons for this are multiple. They may have had greater needs than their parents could meet. The parents may have been inadequate in some way, and this covers a multitude of behaviour, from parents who are too busy, are undemonstrative, prefer a brother or a sister, are too critical, not affectionate enough, and not appreciative enough. For one or some of these reasons, the young person emerges with a hunger for attention. This hunger can last for decades, and the person who takes them on must have the security and capacity to be an affirming spouse for a long time.

Lack of self-esteem

The deprived person is often one who lacks self-esteem, but not necessarily so. The person who lacks self-esteem is apologetic about his or her existence, finds it difficult to believe that they are lovable or wanted by anyone. When approached with intimacy, they are often frightened by it, and they need a lot of reassurance that they are wanted and appreciated.

Anxious attachments

Mention has been made of men and women who make anxious attachments. These individuals are afraid of being abandoned. They are often afraid that the spouse will leave them, and, when anxious attachment is coupled with lack of self-esteem, they torture themselves that someone else will be preferred to them. They tend to spend their time testing those who befriend them to see whether they meant their love. They are rarely reassured and, when satisfied at one level, they put the premium up and subject their partner to even harder tests. These individuals rarely feel safe, and are constantly challenging their partner to love them. They can be most demanding, and anyone who takes them on should be aware of the emotional drain they inflict.

Avoidant attachment

The avoidant attachment individual is a person who relates at arm's length, and is very poor at demonstrating intimacy. When intimacy is needed, with evidence of physical and emotional affection, this is not the person to choose.

Alcohol, gambling, drugs

Whatever the reasons, and there are many, individuals who are prey to alcohol, gambling and drugs, contribute a great deal to marital breakdown. Men and women with a 'rescue' streak in their personality believe they can marry the alcoholic, gambler and drug abuser, and then convert them afterwards to sobriety. This is a great mistake. If such a person is taken on, they should be encouraged to give up their noxious habits before they get married. Even then it should be realised that they can return to these habits after abstinence.

UNCONSCIOUS COLLUSION

The principle of collusion is an unconscious mechanism whereby we tend to choose people like our parents at an unconscious level. If we have been emotionally deprived, one would think that we would select a warm, emotionally giving person, but instead we choose someone who is also inhibited at demonstrating affection. At the unconscious level, we may choose a spouse who is an undemonstrative, critical, demanding, punishing, and generally unrewarding as our unsatisfactory parent has been. We should be on the look-out for unconscious collusion in which we select someone who repeats our adverse parental experience, particularly if our self-esteem is low and we do not feel that we are going to get someone worthwhile or that we do not deserve such a person.

There is no perfect way of testing the personality of the partner we are marrying, but there are certain clues which should put us on our guard. We should get to know the family history of our spouse, and the stability of their childhood. We can learn a great deal from that. We should meet the parents of our future spouse and assess them. It is true we are not marrying our in-laws, but we can learn a great deal from the way they behave and how they are.

Next, we can look at the work record of our partner-to-be. Is it stable and consistent? Work records reveal a great deal of information about an individual. Long periods of unemployment which are not due to social reasons, or too many changes of job are indications of instability.

Have there been broken engagements or a series of previous relationships? That is also indicative of an unstable person.

Apart from the general impression that a person gives, their family, work and previous relationships are a good measure of their stability. When it comes to sexual faithfulness, studies have shown that the more promiscuous a person is before the marriage, the more likely it is that they will be unfaithful afterwards.

ARE YOU SURE?

Finally, I find in counselling that, in many marriages laden with difficulties, one or both partners state that they had persistent doubts from the beginning about the marriage, or that they entered into it knowing fully that they were not in love with their spouse. There is an absolute necessity, as with premarital pregnancy, not to proceed to marriage if there is a persistent lingering doubt about the relationship. In the same way, marriages which are entered into without feeling in love in the hope that time will produce the necessary change should also be resisted.

24

Moral Problems

Many Catholics and Christians of all denominations distance themselves from coming to church and worshipping God because they feel alienated by the rules that the churches impose on sexual behaviour. When they cannot accept the sexual teaching, they feel there is no room for them in that church. The problem becomes more complicated when they are certain that their conduct is right and the Church is wrong. There is little doubt that tension exists between official teaching and the way many people, especially the young, conceive their sexuality, which is one of the most common reasons for alienation from the Church. How is this to be resolved? In this chapter an outline answer is given for each conflict, but some general principles apply in all situations.

Coming to church and worshipping on Sunday and at other times is a recognition that this vast mystery we call the world is not a chance happening but the fruit of a living and loving God who created it out of love and made love the supreme characteristic to be lived in this world and to be shared with the Creator in the next, so that wherever authentic love exists God is present.

Tackling the mystery of creation and deciding whether life is a chance phenomenon or whether we understand its meaning through the wonder of the mystery of creation and the revelation of God in the Old Testament, in his prophets, and finally in Jesus Christ, whose whole life is the ultimate proclamation of love, is the most important issue in our life. On the basis of the answer we give depends the way we run our life, the priorities we choose and the sacrifices we make. If we conclude that we come from nowhere and at death go to oblivion, then there is no reason why we should not concentrate our whole life on pleasure, egoism, money and power, whenever we can get them, short of breaking the law. In those circumstances there is no ultimate basis for human behaviour, and without a God life would become a jungle of the strongest obtaining the maximum gratification at the expense of the weak. A few seconds of reflection of what life would become without a sense of God will horrify us enough to appreciate the importance of this decision in our life.

The alternative, which most people believe, is that there is a God, but they often leave things at that level. Christianity believes not only that there is a God, but that he has revealed himself, lived, died and overcome death. The Church is primarily a sign of this revelation, and we Christians are a community of believers who give testimony to this truth. So going to church and worshipping God is primarily an expression of this belief. In its wisdom the Church makes rules and regulations about human behaviour in its efforts to encourage people to perfect themselves, and to reflect the image of God in them, but these rules and regulations are subordinate to the task of the Church to be the sacrament of Christ.

Although we are bound to take the teaching of the magisterium seriously, rules are not at the centre of being Christian; love is. For one thing, we know that historically some of these rules have changed, but, even if they reflect unchanging truths, obedience to rules is secondary to worshipping God who is the centre of our life. Some Catholics make obedience to the rules appear to be synonymous with worshipping God, sometimes even more important than acknowledging and worshipping God. This is not, of course, the case, and while we must make every effort to obey rules which perfect us, they are not the ultimate criteria of our faith. We have to distinguish what is central in it, which is belief and worship of the Trinity in and through love, and the rules of morality, which assist us in this goal, but are liable to change as knowledge of the truth unfolds.

When it comes to rules which the Church makes, the

Church itself teaches that what we should do is to listen carefully to the teaching, understand and appreciate the truth it is trying to preserve, do our utmost to obey it, but act on the basis of our conscience. An informed conscience is the ultimate judge of how we should behave, even if the decision brings us into conflict with the authority of the Church. If the Church is right, then we are sinners, and the Church has always room for sinners. If it ultimately proves that the Church is wrong in some detail, then we will be justified. There are some Catholics who are horrified at the thought that the Church could be wrong in anything it teaches. Their whole faith is based on obedience to the minutest detail. The fact is that, despite determined efforts to make obedience the supreme virtue, the Church changes its position on many things in the course of history, and is reluctant to make morality a basis for infallible teaching. In fact its teaching on marriage and sexuality before the Second Vatican Council and afterwards is a startling admission of profound changes. This changeability does not make it any less credible because the supreme truth it safeguards is the life, death and resurrection of Jesus Christ.

In summary, therefore, when people find themselves in conflict with the teaching of the Church on moral matters, they should do everything they can to understand this teaching and obey it, but, if their conscience sincerely opposes it they must always follow the latter. Such a conflict, however, is no reason for ceasing to come to worship and acknowledge God.

In the following section the common individual moral issues will be tackled with their moral and personal implications.

DIVORCE

Within the Roman Catholic community the outstanding issue of the last quarter of a century has been contraception. In my view, although the subject is important, it pales into insignificance compared with the rise of divorce.

211

The teaching on divorce comes from Jesus himself, and, as we have seen, is backed in terms of secular research that the consequences are very serious. Everything should be done to prevent it, but if a couple are divorced, how should they approach their lives subsequently?

If a person is divorced, there is no reason why he or she should cease attending the church. Divorce is not a sin; it is remarriage that is forbidden, but frequently the divorced person wants to remarry. This is where the discipline of the Roman Catholic Church and Anglican Church intrudes. The Roman Catholic Church does not permit a remarriage in the church unless an annulment has been obtained from the first marriage. As we have seen already, annulments can be obtained when a husband or wife can be shown to suffer from a grave lack of discretionary judgment concerning the essential matrimonial rights and obligations of the marriage, or because of causes of a psychological nature which stop them from assuming the essential obligations of marriage. A good number of Catholics resort to this relief and marry with the Church's approval the second time around.

What happens when the relief is not available? In these circumstances the divorced Roman Catholic cannot marry in the church, but can do so in a civil ceremony. After that, they can and should attend church. According to official teaching, they are prohibited from receiving Communion, but many people overcome even this obstacle through the medium of their internal forum. At a deeper level there are Roman Catholic theologians who believe that, even in the absence of nullity, second and subsequent marriages are valid in the light of the economia of grace, a theological principle based on Greek Orthodox practice.

Roman Catholic authorities state that the view they take and the accompanying teaching is only made to safeguard marriage. In my view marriage is safeguarded not by penalising the divorced, but by taking a much more active approach, infinitely more active, in supporting marriage.

As far as the Anglican community is concerned, it has yet to sort out the tangle about remarrying its members in church after a divorce.

212

Both communities have spent infinitely more time addressing themselves to the issues of what should happen to the divorced rather than to understanding the present causes of marital turbulence and taking steps to buttress marriage.

CONTRACEPTION

The Catholic Church teaches that birth regulation is moral for good reasons, but only natural means should be employed. At the heart of this teaching is the view that one of the inherent characteristics of sexual intercourse is the procreation of new life, and that every sexual act should therefore remain open to this possibility. This teaching is the most controversial of all the sexual morality of the Catholic Church. Moral theologians are deeply divided about it, and most people neither understand nor follow this teaching. It is also a common source of alienation from the Church.

The alternative point of view is that reproduction belongs to the whole fertile life of a woman, and not to specific moments, particularly as she ovulates only once a month and there is no biological pattern to show that every act of sexual intercourse is open to life. In fact the majority are not.

In the current atmosphere within the Catholic Church, in which obedience to authority is stressed by the magisterium, assent to the teaching on contraception has become an important issue. Nevertheless the majority of young people use contraception, and sadly they feel this excludes them from the Church, which in fact it does not.

One point needs stressing. In the heat of the moral battle, it is often forgotten that there are no perfect contraceptives, and that, at their best, natural methods of family planning are safe and effective and should be seriously considered.

ABORTION

Some protagonists try to put contraception and abortion on the same footing. Clearly the two are very different categories

213

of behaviour. Abortion, for whatever reason, is a serious matter of killing unborn life. The intention of contraception is to use artificial means to prevent conception. The Church teaches that abortion is never justified, a teaching which may appear hard but it protects the most precious human characteristic, which is life. This life is considered to begin from the time of fertilisation, that is, when the ovum and sperm fuse. It is an important and vital safeguard of the unborn, and most Christians treat the teaching with the respect it deserves. Certainly it does not receive the antagonism that the teaching on contraception experiences.

Nevertheless certain circumstances arise out of poverty, a hasty pregnancy which would damage the living children, when it threatens the life of the mother (increasingly less so with advances in medicine), when the baby is handicapped, when the pregnancy is the result of impulsive and irresponsible sexual behaviour, and in other dire situations couples do resort to abortion. The Church teaches that no circumstances justify it, and, as many abortion laws stand, the reasons for termination are usually social.

Every fertilised ovum is potentially reflecting the image of God, and should neither be experimented with nor killed. When either of these events happens, a serious violation of God's creation takes place.

But men and women do fall prey to weaknesses and abortions do occur. Once again there is no reason for leaving the Church.

PREMARITAL SEX AND COHABITATION

A generation ago Christians, and indeed society as a whole, did not have or permit premarital sexual intercourse, nor did they cohabit. Today almost everyone enters marriage having had sexual intercourse, and increasingly couples cohabit for short or long periods. Are they behaving wrongly? In the light of orthodox teaching, yes, but . . .

Let us look at these two behaviours separately. There is a world of difference between casual sexual intercourse and its

214

presence in committed relationships. Sexual intercourse is the sign of the presence of an exclusive, permanent and monogamous relationship between a man and a woman, called marriage. At a late stage in the history of the Church, in the sixteenth century, it was decided that this exclusive, permanent and monogamous relationship, which is called marriage, can only commence when the couple have had a public wedding in the church in the presence of the parish priest and two witnesses. But long before this decision it was the accepted tradition that the ministers of the sacrament of marriage were the couple, and when they decided to commit themselves in a permanent, exclusive and monogamous relationship, they became married, and this marriage was completed by sexual intercourse. So that in having premarital sexual intercourse in the presence of the committed relationship, couples are returning to an earlier situation.

So why all the fuss? The Church's teaching cannot be dismissed lightly. All teaching tries to safeguard some aspect of human integrity. The morality is that the temptation to have sexual intercourse in the absence of exclusiveness, commitment and monogamy is high. The desire of having the pleasure of sex without its personal meaning of love is a constant human problem, and so delaying sexual intercourse until the maximum safeguards of human commitment have been made in the final wedding ceremony is the way that the Church tries to safeguard human integrity. It is not a question that all sex is wrong before the wedding, and right afterwards. Throughout the Church's history sexual intercourse has been a sign of the union between Christ and the Church since the teaching of St Paul in Ephesians 5: 32. It is thus a sign of commitment, permanency, faithfulness and exclusiveness, and whenever these conditions are authentically present sexual intercourse is an appropriate sign of their existence.

The same principles largely apply to cohabitation. Cohabitation, usually of short duration prior to marriage, but sometimes extensive and even permanent, has been escalating in western societies in the last fifteen years. The single most important reason for this is the high rate of divorce. Young people have seen divorce rise to two-thirds of marriages in

215

the USA, and to a lesser, but still high, degree elsewhere. Neither the Church nor society has been able to stem this rise. Young people have taken the matter into their own hands. The simple belief is that, if they live together, they will find out whether they are suited to each other, and a future marriage will last. It is too early to say if this basic aim will be achieved. The evidence so far is not promising, and this is not surprising, given the complexity of marital breakdown.

As far as the morality of cohabitation is concerned, it should be noted that if a couple are committed to an exclusive, permanent, faithful relationship, then they are fulfilling the conditions of marriage. If, on the other hand, they are not experiencing this type of relationship and are simply experimenting, then this is a stage of courtship and a prelude to marriage which contravenes the conditions of permanency as a prerequisite for sexual intercourse. Here we are in unchartered, moral territory which needs careful examination. Does the ultimate good of safeguarding a permanent marriage justify cohabitation?

25

Domestic Church

For from the wedlock of Christians there comes the family, in which new citizens of human society are born. By the grace of the Holy Spirit received in baptism, these are made children of God, thus perpetuating the People of God through the centuries. The family is, so to speak, the domestic Church. (Dogmatic Constitution of the Church, *Lumen Gentrium* II)

The phrase, domestic Church, first appeared in the Second Vatican Council and has since been used in the Apostolic Exhortation, *Familiaris Consortio,* and it is a concept whose importance has not been sufficiently appreciated. For centuries the Christian community has aped the monastery for its spiritual life. Families depart from their home to go to 'church', the physical church of the parish, where prayer and the sacraments are celebrated. There is no focus for the sacrament of marriage. Everything spiritual takes place outside the home. With the increasing demise of church attendance, men and women who have a yearning for God but are alienated from the churches have no way of expressing their living faith.

For those who attend weekly services, and those who only go to church irregularly, we now have a new basis for experiencing God. The domestic Church is a concept rich in spirituality.

It really means that the everyday events which take place in the home are the liturgy of the sacrament of marriage. The heart of this daily experience is loving, and this has been described under sustaining, healing and growth.

Under sustaining, consideration has been given to physical and emotional availability, communication, demonstration of affection and resolution of conflict. That means that every moment the couple spend together, their emotional awareness of each other, their every communication, the demonstration of affection and the resolution of conflict is in fact their prayer life. This is a hard concept to perceive because all these transactions are extremely human ones. This is because the roots of dualism have never been eradicated from the spirituality of the faith. People think that they reach God in an abstract manner when they leave behind their physicality. This is a serious error which alienates men and women from God. What is forgotten is that Christianity is an incarnate faith, and marriage is an ideal expression of divine awareness.

This means that from the moment the couple wake up and begin to communicate, a spiritual transaction is taking place between them. Every moment of their mutual awareness is a moment of prayer. Their physical presence and the words they utter are a mutual salutation of their God-given presence. Communication is much more than utterance of words. It is an attempt at clarity, understanding, affirmation, the desire to be in touch with each other. In the process much effort is spent to make oneself clear and to comprehend what the spouse is saying. As mentioned already, there is a need, not only to spell out meaning in words, but to emphasise, that is, comprehend, via feelings and body signals. We try in ordinary prayer to be in touch with the unseen and the unknown conceptualised as a person. When we are in touch with our spouse and children, we are in contact with the visible representative of the divine, for Christ, whose life we share in the sacrament of marriage, is present in each other, and we are in contact with God minute by minute through physical and emotional presence and communication.

Beyond availability and communication, we demonstrate affection to each other by ordinary politeness and physical expressions of love, through a kiss, hug and an embrace. In the past we have looked at these manifestations as forbidden erotic incidents, and there was no clear manifestation of their spirituality. At their best they were considered legitimate and permitted, but this was a move to rehabilitate them from the clutches of sin. We did not appreciate that they were the stuff out of which spirituality is made. In embracing each other, in making love, couples reach the heart of their love for their special neighbour, who is each other – the era of feeling uncomfortable with these exchanges is over. In the setting of the domestic Church, availability, communication, demonstration of affection and resolution of conflict are the ingredients of the liturgical prayer of the family. Every moment of their day is taken up with some aspect of their expression.

This form of prayer is different from the one to which we are accustomed, where we make the sign of the cross and we address ourselves to the unseen and unknown God. In the liturgical prayer of the family, the unseen and the unknown become the spouse and the children.

The prayer becomes much more intense as the exchange between the members of the family community requires effort, sustained effort and sacrifice. It takes a lot of repeated and sustained effort to communicate effectively, to be genuinely available, show true affection and forgiveness. It is this persistent human endeavour to love and overcome difficulties that is at the heart of the domestic Church.

The domestic Church consists of the couple waking up, dressing, preparing breakfast, taking their children to school, going to work, looking after the home, returning in the evening, having a meal, putting the children to bed, talking to each other, going to bed and making love. The beauty of the theology of the domestic Church is that within it the ordinary becomes extraordinary, and a symbol of saving grace.

There is a need in the theology of marriage to appreciate that the ministers of the sacrament are the couple, and the community of the interacting persons in the family is the domestic Church. They form the visible community of love, and its members are in a continuous worshipping prayer throughout the week.

There is an enormous task ahead converting the idea of the domestic Church into a living theology with the concept that the interaction of the family members is the conversation between themselves and Christ. Just as in the Eucharist there is a living reality of the availability of the body and blood of Christ, so in the sacrament of marriage the availability of the spouses socially, emotionally, sexually, intellectually and spiritually is the basis of recognising Christ in each other. In giving thanks for each other's presence, they are also giving thanks for God in their midst. This is not to say that the family members do not need to go and worship in church – they certainly do – but it does mean that their own abode is a living temple where God is to be found in each other. Every moment of their interaction is a prayer, if by prayer is meant a conscious and deliberate choice to acknowledge and worship God. By acknowledging and worshipping each other as a person, they are recognising Christ in one another. So, of course, how they treat each other matters immensely.

To sum up: the concept of the domestic Church extends the theology of marriage. It brings Christ into the domestic scene, whereby every encounter, from the most trivial to the most profound, is a form of living prayer between the members of the family community. Every home is a power base of prayer, expressed through the minute-to-minute interaction of its members. The family no longer needs to imitate the monastic life. It has a liturgy of its own in which the family members are assembled daily in the events of family life. This community of love then takes the fruits of its love to the wider community of the parish at the Sunday Eucharist.

26

Evangelisation

The 1990s have been selected as the decade of evangelisation. This is a challenging issue. The revolution that Jesus Christ brought about two thousand years ago has to continue and be handed over from age to age. Survey after survey has shown that ours is an age with a high belief in the concept of God and a very low interest in the practice of faith. This is a phenomenon of urban societies, but it also affects the rural parts of the country. Part of the problem is the breakdown of community life. The community supports and fosters a sense of togetherness which shares the mysteries of life and seeks a transcendental explanation. This transcendental notion is not lost in urban life, but is diluted by an immense impersonality. The assembly point of the urban world is the bus, train, the pub, the football match, not the church. The meeting points do not offer an opportunity to learn about your neighbour, to familiarise oneself with their difficulties, challenges and pains. There is no easy way of access of love, and so there is no shifting of the horizons to a transcendental reality.

Instead there is a quest for information, a seeking of answers which are looked for in science. We are living in an age which is obsessed with factuality. It wants to know how things work. The challenge to pain is not to respond to a person but to remove the pain. Everything untidy has to be made tidy and orderly, even though in the process we create chaos through pollution. Fascinating as science is, the technological answers to problems which bypass humanity cannot answer the deepest needs of human nature. Materialism is an important illusion because no matter how clever science is, it cannot satisfy the hunger for human experience. The moment to moment experience of being human is an exhilaration that cannot be contained by the practicalities of living reality. The thirst for information and technological advance is certainly temporarily overwhelming human beings, but it does not answer the complexity of being human. Science, of course, cannot be underrated. It has given us the means of exploring the mystery of life, but the answers do not exhaust the mystery.

This is where the churches are also failing. The traditional services, sermons and vision have failed to capture the deepening insights of human nature. A century of dynamic psychology has revolutionised our understanding of human interaction which has hardly touched Christian thought. We have a real problem in which human experience has deepened but the network of Christian services has not accompanied the depths of the changes. This is not because the gospels have not got the insights to accompany the psychological depths, but because Christianity has not learned to use the social sciences effectively. By generally adopting a superior attitude to the social sciences and not integrating them in Christianity, the latter has yet to realise a unique opportunity for evangelisation.

A unique opportunity for evangelisation is to be found in contemporary marriage. As has been shown throughout this book, there is a convergence between a secular quest for love in marriage and a religious understanding of love. The religious interest is as old as the Judaeo-Christian tradition in which love has played a prominent part, and in Christianity God has been revealed as love. Love then is an unconscious seeking by western society for God who is repudiated in the institutional churches. It is the task of Christianity to help reconcile the understanding of love, which has emerged from our secular explorations, with the inheritance received from Christianity. This is the task of the next and final chapter of the book.

In the process of reconciling the two aspects of love, Christianity has a unique opportunity to evangelise. It is taking on a ready-made interest of the secular world, namely love in personal relationships. Instead of examining in detail where these relationships go wrong and contradict religious tradition, the churches should be looking excitedly at the new opportunities afforded by this new trend.

Some of this love involves areas which have been notoriously difficult for Christianity. At least two aspects, namely sexuality and the erotic, and the position of women in society, have been stumbling blocks for Christian thought. Now is the opportunity to move forward. As far as sexuality is concerned, we have come to a point where the traditional link between sex and children is nearly over. We are entering a new exciting era of investigating the inner world of eroticism, and the link between sexual activity and personal integrity. Christianity is strong on personal integrity but weak on valuing eroticism, and a new synthesis is urgently needed which will raise human sexuality to a new level of spirituality. The same applies to the emerging status of women who have to be treated, as Jesus treated them, on an equal basis with men. The inner world of love, eroticism, and the relationship between men and women, is a fruitful area for a new era of spirituality within the family.

This emphasis on the inner world of the family threatens those who are not married, the single, the separated and divorced, and the widowed. The fact is that all these people are part of family life, and have spent large parts of their life in family settings; but an emphasis on marriage and family life is not meant to be an inward looking, self-centred love. On the contrary, a real understanding of loving within the family reveals a depth of Christian love which spills over into the world outside the home. When spouses and their children are sensitised to love in depth in their personal relationships, then they are aware of their neighbour with much greater perspicacity.

In this way the inner world of the family, with its emphasis on love, becomes the basis of the Christian gospel. The domestic Church is the liturgical life of its members. Through a natural basis of normal attraction, men and women and their children become aware of God through their love of each other.

The idea of evangelising through the family shocks those

223

who take delight in being busy outside the home. It is much easier to be concerned with the poor in many parts of the world, and in the community within which one lives, than to work week after week for a better understanding within the home. Working with strangers is highly attractive because it does not mobilise the intimate parts of our personality with which we have difficulties. Many people can get a pseudo sense of holiness by dealing with those outside the home rather than relating to their family. Yet it is the nearest relative that offers the most persistent challenge of love.

This has been poignantly demonstrated in the wave of divorce that has swept western societies in the last thirty years. As the West has to face the intensity of intimacy in personal relations, so it has caved in with overwhelming difficulties. Without ignoring the world outside the family, we have to focus on the inner world of personal relationships. This is not so much because we have to fight divorce, but rather because we have to learn to love more deeply. This love engages a world of intimacy in feelings and emotions, and goes well beyond social relations. This is precisely what our Lord taught – that love is a majestic output of the heart, well beyond the law of his day. That is precisely the challenge of our day, to go into the depths of feelings that are the background of sustaining, healing and growth.

The problem with seeing love in terms of God is the fear that human love alone is no more than complete humanism. Everybody loves. Where is God to be found in that? The answer is that, if we take our faith seriously, then in the depths of love we invariably find God:

> My dear friends,
> If God loves us so much,
> we too should love each other.
> No one has ever seen God,
> but as long as we love each other
> God remains in us
> and his love comes to its perfection in us.
>
> (1 John 4:11–12)

Christians are accustomed to being told to love their neighbour; they hear this weekly in their church. What they are not used to is the idea that in loving they find God in each other. The simple experience of loving is loaded with so much energy that it becomes God-driven. Love carries such intensity that it radiates the whole of our being, and in this way transforms us into a God-like state. This does not mean that in loving we have a sufficiency of God's presence. Loving makes us aware of God; it fires our imagination and it motivates us, but in the end we have to be aware of God as a person, and the ideal of spirituality in the home is a life laden with love which personifies God, and this divine person motivates us to love even more deeply. It is a positive cycle of love which is the opposite side of the negative cycle of human relations in which men and women do not love enough, become alienated and then love even less.

In meeting the challenge of contemporary intimacy in personal relations, commentators have focused on the high rate of divorce, the level of cohabitation, the extramarital births in a summary of negation. I would rather suggest that contemporary intimacy is an invitation to put the perennial Christian command of love to the service of humanity. The agape of the gospel needs to join hands with the love that is emerging from the social sciences, particularly psychology, to offer a new wave of evangelisation in our midst.

The opportunity is there to grasp in our society which is alienated from the institutional churches but hungry to explore the meaning of God. What better opportunity to present God other than as a source of love in personal relationships? The whole gospel is an odyssey of love in personal relationships, and we have a unique opportunity in our day and time to explore this theme.

This could lead to a return to church practice by helping people to see that they worship the God they are seeking in the midst of their family, and that on Sunday they can encounter the same mystery in the parochial church.

But whether or not we worship God on Sunday in the parochial church, a raising of the awareness of God as love will be a fitting way to take up the challenge of evangelisation.

27

Contemporary Loving

This book has attempted to examine the internal shift of marriage from an institution for the begetting and raising of children to primarily an interpersonal relationship of love of the spouses, out of which the energy for conceiving and educating the children will arise. We are in the midst of this change, and we need to understand and appreciate it in depth if we are to reduce the colossal damaging impact of marital breakdown. In these last three chapters I have outlined a vision for the Christian community to take the new challenge of marriage seriously and make it the focus of the domestic church, evangelisation and the thrust of Christian love.

I shall start by stating what I understand are the traditional secular and religious values concerning marriage and the family to be. Marriage was seen primarily to be for children and the energy of the spouses to be expended in raising them up. Their interpersonal relationship was of secondary importance. Their togetherness was action-orientated in structuring a partnership of the man to be the centre of action as a provider and head of the family, and the wife as a begetter and raiser of children. This inner world of marriage focused on children, and the time before their arrival and after their departure was hazy. The relationship of the couple was subordinate to the needs of the children.

Within this framework of marriage, the difficulties that arose in the marriage were largely understood as an expression of selfishness. This traditional view is expressed to this very day, as evil is fully understood by the egoism of the people concerned. The selfishness was further explained by lack of self-control, and in sexual matters as lack of suppression of instincts. Suppression was the normal order of the day. Between them, control and suppression dictated all conduct and behaviour. Things were not talked through, they were controlled. Anger, violence, drink, sex, were all to be suppressed. This applied particularly to sexual matters, which were a particular object of suppression.

When things went wrong, the way to change them was by allocating wrongdoing to one partner or the other, accepting blame and seeking forgiveness. The supreme Christian weapon was to forgive the guilty party. An essential part of understanding human relationships was the need to find a 'bad' and 'good' spouse and allocate badness and goodness respectively. There was no point beyond forgiveness except to tolerate what could not be changed. This attitude was reinforced by the popular belief that people could not change, and there was no point in trying to alter or expecting change in one's spouse. Spouses settled for compromise and did not, except on rare occasions, proceed to divorce or separation.

If we are to understand what is happening to marriage, we have to learn that all these traditional values are in the process of being altered.

Marriage is changing from an institution largely devoted to raising children to an interpersonal relationship of intimacy, in which couples seek the realisation of their potential and maximum fulfilment of feelings and sexuality. Children are raised and nurtured, but the strength of their total education is being derived from the interpersonal energy sustained by the relationship. There is a good deal of tension between the priorities of the interpersonal relationship and the needs of the children.

The emphasis on the interpersonal relationship stems from the breakdown of clearly delineated roles of the spouses to a world in which women are covering many of the same areas as men. This has shifted the world of men and women from a togetherness based on action to an intimacy based on availability, communication and feelings. In this shift, men have suffered from a loss of closely delineated roles, and have been invited to enter the woman's world of words and feelings, in which the latter has distinct advantages. Loving here has

227

shifted from action to quality of relationship, and there is an emphasis on sustaining, healing and growth, all of which will be mentioned below.

The traditional answer to marital difficulties of selfishness is giving way to a desire to be understood psychologically. Why am I behaving in this way? Why are you behaving in that way? These have become the natural quests instead of resorting to a primordial original sin expressed in selfishness. Men and women are hungry to be understood and to be responded to accurately instead of being dismissed as 'bad'. A hundred years of psychology of all types, but particularly the dynamic variety, has transformed human horizons. Instead of being indicted, spouses long to be reached in the depths of their being, and to be helped in as many ways as possible to realise their potential. Dynamic psychology has made us aware that there is a reason for our behaviour. We want to reach the reasons for our behaviour and to be helped to overcome the difficulties. We long to be healed and to grow. We do not want to be labelled as 'bad' and thrown on the heap of human dirt. We long to have our origins appreciated, our vulnerabilities recognised, respected and possibly remedied.

In the past the best that we could hope for was to be humble enough, acknowledge our faults and ask to be forgiven, but at the moment of forgiveness we remained labelled as guilty. It was the magnanimity of our spouse that forgave us. Modern men and women know enough of psychology to appreciate that their behaviour is up to a point determined, and they are not as responsible as their indicters would like to make them. They long for a human relationship which goes beyond human forgiveness to the restoration of their human integrity. They long for their spouse to understand them and to help them be restored to a fuller sense of their potential. They do not want to be stuck with a magnanimous spouse who forgives but retains their superiority over them.

Contemporary spouses have higher expectations of each other. In particular, women expect so much more from men. These high expectations in the quality of the relationship have come to stay. They are a permanent feature of the fabric of the man-woman encounter. Theologically, instead of being seen as unrealistic feminist aspirations, they can be considered as the quest of both sexes for a realisation of the image of God, not by denial and limitations, but by a plenitude of being.

In this quest, sacrifice is needed. This is where Christianity can make a specific contribution. Healing and growth cannot be achieved in a moment. They take a lifetime of achievement, but sacrifice now is not a static entity. It is no longer acquiescence to the inevitable. Sacrifice is required to pursue in depth the personality of the partner, and to help them overcome their difficulties. Instead of dismissing one's spouse with 'what can you expect from him or her? He or she is always like that. That's how he/she is', spouses want to be helped to deepen their personality. Sacrifice is the equivalent of the patience of the therapist who waits and helps the patient to change.

Spouses are no longer prepared to put up with impossible spouses. Of course, it all depends on what is interpreted as an 'impossible' spouse. Western societies have to learn that, by giving up one spouse they are not buying a ticket to heavenly bliss with the next partner. They are right in insisting on change, but loving implies a prolonged period of waiting, in which there is active change, and they have a role to play in that change, by encouraging, affirming and praising the efforts their partner makes to change.

Spouses want to change the traditional concept of 'putting up' with unacceptable behaviour. They want to minimise what they 'put up with'. The whole ethos of contemporary human relationship is a realisation of human integrity, not a denial and suppression of the unacceptable. Christianity can only rejoice at this quest for wholeness. It needs to show that loving is not to be achieved by denial and suppression but by a lifetime's exploration whereby behaviour can be changed. The aim is to change positively here on earth. This means that Christians have to emphasise this world as a place of human perfection, and not to treat it as a vale of tears with a rich reward in the world to come. Human beings are hungry

229

for perfection here and now, and their biggest opportunity to realise it is in their interpersonal relationships.

To sum up this section on interpersonal loving, we are witnessing a phase in human relationships in which men and women are seeking human integrity in the presence of each other. Being understood and responded to accurately is the key to loving. At its best Christianity forgives and accepts the limitations of one's spouse. This is superb, but it is no longer enough. We have to take heed of the teaching of our Lord, who coupled forgiveness with the injunction to 'sin no more'. 'Sinning no more' is really realising one's potential and integrity. Spouses are anxious to find their potential and integrity from each other. They want their partner to understand them and facilitate their healing and growth. That is why we have to impart to our children a deeper insight as to how men and women function, so that in the depths of their intimacy, they can reach out to the hurt child in each other and heal it.

Loving implies a process of never-ending healing and growth, and there cannot be any finer goal for Christian spirituality. There has to be a fundamental shift in Christian thought from explaining everything in terms of selfishness to a genuine understanding of the needs of the other and responding to them.

All this applies to interpersonal love, but we must also appreciate that there has been a radical shift in sexuality. For nearly two thousand years sex has been allied to procreation. It has to be realised that that era is over. Sexual intercourse is now unequivocally an expression of love, combining the erotic with the personal. Christianity has to embrace this point of view. It has no difficulty in understanding the importance of personal love, but it must take the plunge and rejoice in the erotic. Then it can help society realise that the fullness of sexuality is to be found in the conjunction between the erotic and the personal. The world is besotted with the erotic but is not so strong on personal love, and there is much emphasis on the transient realisation of pleasure. Christianity, which has a weak grasp of the momentous importance of the erotic, plays it down and tries to emphasise personal love. In the past it emphasised procreation. It is necessary for the erotic and the personal to join forces and become mutually significant. Christianity has to appreciate that sexual instincts are not to be suppressed, but confined to personal loving, and society has to realise that unfettered sexual instincts do not represent authentic human behaviour. In this way lack of self-esteem is translated into fullness of being and self-esteem.

Christianity has to recognise the shifts in the internal world of marriage from children to spouses, from a patriarchal point of view to an equality of worth of the sexes, from a togetherness based on activity and social roles to an intimacy of love.

This book aims to encourage Christianity to move beyond the first halting steps of understanding marriage as a community of love to actually fleshing out what that love is in terms of interpersonal needs and sexuality.

If we are to do this in our schools, churches and the community, a new dawn of Christian marriage will emerge in which the domestic church and evangelisation will be its manifestation, and a new spring of love will emerge from the ashes of marital breakdown and divorce.